The Little Black Book of Project Management

Third Edition

Michael C. Thomsett

American Management Association

New York • Atlanta • Brussels • Buenos Aires • Chicago • London • Mexico City
San Francisco • Shanghai • Tokyo • Toronto • Washington, D.C.

Special discounts on bulk quantities of AMACOM books are available to corporations, professional associations, and other organizations. For details, contact Special Sales Department, AMACOM, a division of American Management Association, 1601 Broadway, New York, NY 10019.
Tel: 800-250-5308. Fax: 518-891-2372.
E-mail: specialsls@amanet.org
Website: www.amacombooks.org/go/specialsales
To view all AMACOM titles go to: www.amacombooks.org

Library of Congress Cataloging-in-Publication Data

Thomsett, Michael C.
    The little black book of project management / Michael C. Thomsett.—3rd ed.
        p.   cm.
    Includes bibliographical references and index.
    ISBN-13: 978-0-8144-1529-0
    ISBN-10: 0-8144-1529-6
    1. Project management.   I. Title.
HD69.P75T48   2009
658.4'04—dc22   2009012803

Printing number

10 9 8 7 6 5 4 3 2

Contents

American Management Association
www.amanet.org

List of Figures

Introduction to the Third Edition

It is your business when the
wall next door catches fire.

—HORACE—

Getting more results with fewer resources: This ideal defines project initiatives in many organizations. However, it is not simply the economic value, efficiency, or speed that defines success in project management. The process needs also to involve quality control in the supply chain, concern for product safety and value, and cooperation within the organization.

Project management is appropriate for any nonrecurring, complex, and costly assignment. If a team is going to include participants who cross departmental and sector lines and who may even involve project managers with lower corporate rank than some team members, then a specialized team structure is essential. This also has to involve developing a carefully defined overall plan, choosing the right team, preparing a project budget, and creating a realistic and executable schedule. The coordination of a project is complex and demands mastery over many kinds of variables.

Imagine this situation: You have been named as project manager for a nonrecurring, complex, and potentially costly project. You know immediately that the degree of your success in completing this project is going to impact your career. Typically, your resources are going to be limited, your budget too small, and the deadline too short. Also typically, management has defined this project in terms of the desired end result but not including the method of execution.

This assignment challenges your management, leadership, and organizational skills. A manager or supervisor can control and execute recurring tasks within a limited department or even in a multidepartmental sector, as long as those routines recur in a manner that is known in advance, with potential risks easily identified, quantified, and mitigated. This situation is rare, however. Such a simple responsibility might seem desirable, but there are the variables—the things you don't anticipate—that go wrong and that make organizational life interesting. This is more so in project management than in departmental, sector, or divisional management.

A project assignment may be defined as (a) outside of your normal responsibilities, (b) involving nonrecurring tasks, and (c) involving team members or resource providers outside of your immediate organizational realm of operation. As soon as you are put in charge of a project or asked to serve as a team member, your first question might be, "What is this project supposed to accomplish?" You are likely to discover that no one knows the answer. The project might be simplistic in definition, with the desired end result identified, but lacking the benefits it provides, the means for accomplishing it, or even the systems to sustain it once completed. Many projects are defined not specifically, but in terms of "results." For example, your project might be to "reduce the defects in a process," "reduce the cost of providing service," or "speed up the time it takes to deliver goods to the market."

These end-result definitions are not actually definitions at all. They are end results, perceived improvements over the current system. So as project manager or team member, you are really not given any guidance about what has to be changed or fixed. The project team's first responsibility is going to be to identify a *plan* that begins with the assigned end result and tracks back through the system to determine how problems are going to be addressed.

This *Little Black Book* is intended as a guide to help you manage or take part in any project. This means, by necessity, that you need to determine how to define what needs to be achieved at every level within a project process. To do this, the overall project has to be broken

down into smaller, more manageable phases. This is how any complicated task has to be addressed. Trying to attack the whole job at once
is not only impossible and disorganized, it will also lead to an unsatis-
factory result. The only way to control budgets and schedules is to define logical starting points *and* stopping points, helping lead the team
to successful completion. This includes reaching not only the goals imposed on you at the time of project assignment (the end result) but
other goals the team sets as well (reduced costs, faster processing,
lower errors, better internal controls). This approach also helps you to
anticipate problems in a coming project phase and to take steps to
address them. Another advantage is that it will help to define concrete
objectives in addition to the stated end result.

Projects may also be long term due to their complexity and impact.
This causes even the best organized managers to experience difficulty
in managing projects. But if you know how to organize and manage
recurring tasks, you already understand the common problems associated with the work cycle, staffing issues, and budgetary restraints. Your
skill in working with these restrictions qualifies you also to manage
projects. The project environment is different, but your skills are applicable.

The context of a project is different from the recurring routines
you deal with every day. First, because the project involves nonrecurring tasks and problems, their solutions cannot be anticipated or managed routinely; you are going to need to develop solutions creatively
and in cooperation with team members. Second, unlike well-defined
tasks you are accustomed to, projects are likely to cross lines of responsibility, authority, and rank, thereby introducing many new problems.
Third, a project plan extends over many weeks or months, so you need
to develop and monitor a budget and schedule for longer than the
normal monthly cycle. Most managers are used to looking ahead for a
matter of days or weeks for a majority of their routines, but projects
demand a longer-term perspective.

The application of skills has to occur in a different environment,
but you already possess the basic management tools to succeed in managing a project. Your ability to plan, organize, execute, respond to the
unexpected, and to *solve* all work for projects as they work within a

more predictable work environment. They only need to be applied with greater flexibility and in a range of situations you cannot anticipate or predict. The project may be defined as an exception to the rules of operation. It demands greater diligence in terms of budgets and schedules, and, of course, you will no doubt be expected to continue with your regularly recurring routines in addition to working through the project.

Operating a project is like starting a new division or department. You have no historical budget as a starting point, no known cycle to add structure as you move through routines, and no way to anticipate scheduling problems. You do not even have a known range of problems needed to be addressed, because everything about the project is new.

Think of this *Little Black Book* as a collection of basic information you need, not only as you proceed through your project but also to create a foundation for the project-based structure you are going to create. That structure relies on organization, style, character, and arrangement of resources, and *you* will play a central role in defining, drawing upon, and applying these resources. The project is also going to demand the application of essential management skills, including leadership and anticipating coming problems. This book shows you how to take charge of even the most complex project and proceed with confidence in yourself and your project team.

This third edition expands on the material in previous editions by incorporating many new elements. In addition, this edition includes the current fusion of traditional project management with the widely practiced and effective skills of Six Sigma, a discussion of how value chain applies to all projects and processes, and referrals to many online resources, notably software for project management. The intention of this new edition is not only to continue to expand on the advice and application of sound management principles you need as a project manager, but also to help you develop your own internal systematic approach in applying your experience in a project environment.

1

Organizing for the Long Term

*Never tell people how to do things. Tell them what to do
and they will surprise you with their ingenuity.*

—GEORGE S. PATTON—

The new clerk in the mailroom noticed an elderly gentleman sitting
in a corner, slowly sorting through a mountain of mail.

"Who's that?" he asked the supervisor.

"That's old Charlie. He's been with the company more than forty
years."

The new clerk asked, "Are you saying he never made it out of the
mailroom?"

"He did, but then he asked to be transferred here—after spending
a few years as a project manager."

Dread. That is a common reaction most managers have to being given
a project assignment. Few managers will seek out the project, and most
will avoid it if possible. Why?

First, a distinction has to be made between projects and routines. The routines associated with operation of your department are repetitive in nature. Put another way, they are predictable. That means that the recurring operations you execute can be planned as a matter of course. Once you have gone through your normal cycle a few times, you know what to expect. Because they are predictable, recurring operational routines that are easier to manage than projects.

The project itself is temporary and nonrecurring in nature. It has a beginning and an end rather than a repetitive cycle. Thus, projects are by nature chaotic. Making projects even more daunting is that few companies have specialized project teams or departments. The project is assigned to a manager who seems to be a logical choice for the job. If the project is related to marketing, it will probably be assigned within the marketing area of the company. If financial in nature, the accounting or internal auditing department will be likely candidates.

Project scope and duration are impossible to define because projects arise at every level within the organization. This characteristic presents special problems for every manager because merely receiving a project assignment does not necessarily mean that you know what will be involved in the task. This makes scheduling and budgeting difficult, to say the least. A project has to be planned out, defined, and organized before you can know what you are up against in terms of actual management. Thus, you may be given an assignment, budget, and deadline before the project itself has been defined well enough to proceed. It will then be necessary to revise not only the schedule and budget, but perhaps the very definition of the project itself.

The secret to the skilled execution of a project is not found in the development of new skills, but in applying existing skills in a new environment. Projects are exceptional, out of the ordinary, and by definition, temporary in nature. So the problems, restrictions, deadlines, and budget are all outside the normal course of your operations. Some professions deal in projects continuously; for example, engineers, contractors, and architects operate in a project environment for every job they undertake. However, they have the experience to manage any problem that arises because it is part of their "skills package" to operate in ever-changing circumstances where similar problems arise.

You manage a series of problems in your department as an operational fact of life. Your department may be defined in terms of the kinds of problems you face each month and overcome. The controls you apply, budgets you meet, and reports you generate as a result of confronting problems within your operational cycle are the outcomes you know and expect. Assignments are made in the same or similar time sequence from month to month, and routines are performed in the same order, usually by the same employees. Even many of the problems that arise are predictable. However, when you are faced with the temporary and exceptional project, it raises several questions, all of which are related to questions of organization, planning, and control. These include:

How do I get started?

Exactly what is the project meant to achieve or discover?

Who is responsible for what, and how is the effort to be coordinated?

Beyond these are the equally important questions related to budgets, schedules, and assignments to a project team. The project presents a set of new demands that, although temporary in nature, require commitment from limited resources. Your department will be expected to continue meeting its recurring work schedule. Thus, a project places an additional burden on you and the others in your department. If the project also involves working with people in other departments, it will create even more potential problems. The point at which responsibility and work processes occur between departments often is also the point at which the smooth processing of the project routine is likely to be disrupted.

Background for Project Management

The difficulties you face as a project manager can be made to conform with a logical system for planning and execution, even when you need to continue managing your department at the same time. Much thought has gone into the science of project management on many levels. If you work regularly in a project environment, you can find

American Management Association
www.amanet.org

assistance and support from several sources, including the Project Management Institute (PMI).

This book adheres to the standards expressed by the Project Management Institute and attempts to present readers with a concise overview of the principles they'll need to employ as project manager. To begin, it is important to define some of the basic principles and ideas underlying the work of project management.

Spotlight on Project Management Institute (PMI)

The Project Management Institute has 265,000 members in 170 countries and was founded in 1969. PMI offers certificate programs for the credentials Project Management Professional (PMP), Certified Associate of Project Management (CAPM), Program Management Professional (PgMP), PMI Scheduling Professional (PMI-SP), and PMI Risk Management Professional (PMI-RM P).

PMI also publishes *A Guide to the Project Management Body of Knowledge*. This useful guide, often referred to as the *PMBOK*, compiles information from many sources. It has incorporated many of the standards established by project management writers, including information from the first and second editions of *The Little Black Book of Project Management* (1990 and 2002). PMBOK was first published in 1996 with revised editions in 2000 and 2004. Contact PMI at:

14 Campus Boulevard
Newtown Square PA 19073–3299
Phone: 610–336–4600
E-mail: customercare@pmi.org
Website: www.pmi.org

Other Resources

To find local PMI chapters, check the PMI website and link to "Community Membership" and then to "Chapter." All local chapters are listed.

Project Definitions

The project is best defined in two ways:

1. By comparing a project to a routine

2. By knowing the operational constraints associated with projects

A "project" has different meanings in each organization and may also vary from one department to another. For the purposes of proceeding with the preliminary steps in organizing your project, this book adheres to the two-part definition mentioned above: by comparison to routines and by the constraints under which projects are run.

The comparison between projects and routines can be divided into four parts as summarized in Figure 1-1 and outlined here:

1. *A project is an exception.* Unlike routines, projects involve investigation, compilation, arrangement, and reporting of findings in some way that provides value. The answers to the basic project questions cannot be found in the routines of your department, which is

Figure 1-1. Comparing projects and routines.

Project	Routine
Exception to the usual range of functions.	Defined within the scope of the department.
Activities are related.	Routines are related.
Goals and deadlines are specific.	Goals and deadlines are general.
The desired result is identified.	No singular result is identified.

what makes it exceptional. The processes involved with the project fall outside your department's "normal" range of activities and functions.

2. *Project activities are related, regardless of departmental routines.* Projects are rarely so restricted in nature that they involve only one department. The characteristics of a department involve related routines, but projects are not so restricted. Thus, a project is likely to involve activities that extend beyond your immediate department, which also means that your project team may include employees from other departments.

3. *Project goals and deadlines are specific.* Recurring tasks invariably are developed with departmental goals in mind. Financial departments crunch numbers, marketing departments promote sales and develop new markets, and filing departments organize paperwork. The goals and related tasks tend to move forward primarily in terms of time deadlines. The same is true for departmental deadlines; they are recurring and dependable, tied to specific cyclical dates or events in other departments. Projects, though, have an isolated and finite number of goals that do not recur, plus identifiable starting and stopping points. Whereas departmental routines are general in nature, project activities are clearly specific.

4. *The desired result is identified.* A project is well defined only when a specific result is known. By comparison, departmental routines involve functions that may be called "process maintenance." That means that rather than producing a specific outcome, a series of recurring routines are aimed at ensuring the flow of outcomes (e.g., reports) from one period to another. The department gets information from others, processes it, and passes it on in a refined form, and this series of steps takes place continuously. While a project involves the same basic idea—receiving information, analyzing it, and reporting conclusions—there are two clear distinctions worth keeping in mind. First, the work is nonrecurring, so the demands of a project cannot be easily identified in every case. Second, the desired result is identified in isolation from other functions of the department.

Projects are also distinguished from routines by how they operate under the constraints of result, budget, and time (see Figure 1-2).

To a degree, all management functions operate within these constraints. For example, your department probably is expected to perform and produce one or more results, or outcomes; you operate within a specific budget; and by the nature of your work, you prioritize on the basis of deadlines. Without these constraints, a company would lack definition and order. We may also judge a company or department by how well it adheres to the expectations for results, budget, and time.

The same is true for projects. The constraints under which you operate also provide a means for testing and judging quality of work. The constraints, whether applied to your department or to a one-time project, are perpetual. However, emphasis on the three constraints is not always applied at the same level; some variation of emphasis should be expected, depending on the nature of the project or the work of a department.

The priority given to one constraint or another is demonstrated as part of a departmental routine. The constraints are constant and part of the nature of the work being performed in each case. However, a project, unlike a department, will succeed or fail purely on the basis of the three constraints as follows:

1. *Result.* Completion of a specific, defined task or a series of tasks is the primary driving force behind the project. Unlike the recur-

Figure 1-2. Three project constraints.

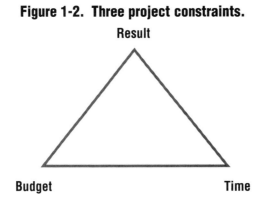

ring tasks that are faced on the departmental level, the project is targeted to the idea of a finite, one-time result.

2. *Budget.* A project's budget is separate from the department's budget. The project team operates with a degree of independence in terms of control and money (even though each team member may be expected to continue completion of departmental tasks). Project teams may include individuals from several different departments; thus, budgetary controls cannot always be organized along departmental lines. A project may require a capital budget as well as an expense budget. As project manager, you may also have more than the usual amount of control over variances.

3. *Time.* Projects have specific starting and ending points. A well-planned project is based on careful controls over completion phases, which involves careful use of each team member's time.

Definition and Control

In organizing your project within the aforementioned limitations, you must also master two components that characterize every project. To complete the project successfully, you need to define, and to control, each aspect of the project itself. Without definition and control, you will be less likely to achieve (or know) the desired final result, within budget, and by the deadline.

As illustrated in Figure 1-3, the definition component of the project is the proper starting point that leads through to the control phase.

Elements That Define a Project

■ ***Purpose.*** What is the expectation? Why is the project being undertaken? What conclusions or answers to problems is it expected to produce?

■ ***Tasks.*** How can a large project be broken down into a series of short-term progress steps? A large project can be overwhelming,

Figure 1-3. Defining and controlling the project.

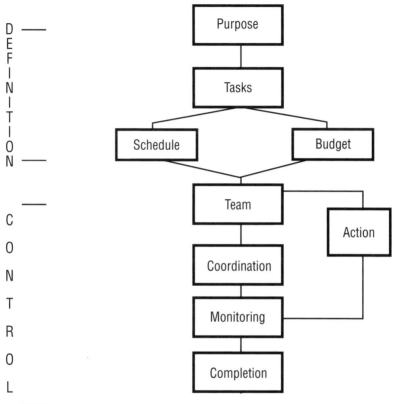

D ——
E
F
I
N
I
T
I
O
N ——

——

C

O

N

T

R

O

L

——

whereas smaller steps can be attacked methodically and completed according to a schedule.

▪ ***Schedule.*** What is the final deadline? With that deadline in mind, how should a series of smaller tasks be arranged, maintained, and timed? Effective task scheduling is the key to meeting longer-term deadlines.

▪ ***Budget.*** How much should the project cost? Will the company need to invest in research, capital equipment, promotion, or market testing? What expenses will be involved, and how much money needs to be set aside for final completion? Will you be expected to complete all or part of the project within your existing departmental budget, and is that expectation realistic?

Elements That Control a Project

▪ **Team.** You will not always be able to organize your team from your own department alone. However, before building a team, you need to develop project definitions so that you know the scope of the project.

▪ **Coordination.** By its nature, the project demands consistent and firm management. Committees do not work well if they are overly democratic, so as project manager you need to have complete responsibility for pulling together the efforts of everyone on the project team.

▪ **Monitoring.** Your schedule and budget will succeed only if you are able to spot emerging problems and correct them. Delegating work to others and creating a control system are essential, but they are only starting points. You also need to track the indicators that reveal whether your project is on schedule and within budget. So much of the job of project manager involves piloting the project that it may be your primary action; an especially complex project requires that monitoring be a constant.

▪ **Action.** If you discover that scheduling or budgetary problems are developing, action should be taken immediately to reverse those trends. If the team is falling behind schedule, the pace of work has to be accelerated. (Or, if it turns out that the original schedule was unrealistic, it should be revised right away.) If your expenses are exceeding budget, additional controls should be put into place to avoid further variances. These steps are possible only when you take action as soon as problems are discovered.

▪ **Completion.** Even when the project is effectively managed and kept on schedule for 99 percent of the time, if the final step is not taken the deadline will not be met. Even well-run projects sometimes prove difficult to close out. The final report or recommendation, the commitment to paper, often proves to be the hardest part of the entire project.

A New Look for Project Management

Project management is a *dynamic* process, and new ideas are continually entering into the methods of practice. Today's organization looks much different from the organization a decade ago, due to many factors: the Internet, information technology (IT), changing cultural beliefs, enlightened social ideas, and even experimental management techniques.

Among the trends affecting how your project will operate are four key areas:

1. *Six Sigma.* The management ideal has changed dramatically since widespread acceptance and use of Six Sigma. This important quality approach is not only a systematic way to tackle quality issues, but also a revised organizational culture. The inclusionary aspects of Six Sigma have vastly changed how many organizations work, including most of the Fortune 500 companies, federal and state governments, branches of the military, and not-for-profit companies. Six Sigma cannot be isolated from project management because it offers a framework for ensuring value and permanence in the output resulting from the project. Chapter 2 explains Six Sigma from a project management perspective.

2. *Risk management.* The concept of risk management has in the past been isolated to a rather one-dimensional view of risk itself. *Risk* used to be defined as something to be mitigated through insurance, passed on to vendors or other operating segments, or simply ignored as something unlikely to occur. Today, with an increased awareness of the expanded realm of threats, this has changed. Today, identity theft, automated system hacking, terrorism, internal sabotage, corporate espionage, pandemics, and natural disasters are but a few of the types of risks that—while always having been there—are now being more widely accepted as real and serious problems in every organization. The increased reliance on vendors overseas (often very few in number but originating in one country) augment the risks that organizations face from political unrest, strikes, transportation slowdown or disasters, and product quality control at the source.

Today, project managers have to expect to include risk management as one of the important attributes to be built into revised and improved processes and internal controls. This incorporates the concept of the *value chain*, which, like the supply chain, describes how a process evolves from start to finish. The value chain is intended as a method for building quality throughout a process, while also mitigating and preventing known risks. The value chain is the topic of Chapter 9.

3. *Virtual project execution and integration.* In the past, a project team normally included individuals with specific skills and experience in a closely defined area of function within an organization. This was necessary due to the limitations of communication before the Internet. So projects either were usually in one place or required travel, telephone meetings, or breakdowns of single projects into geographically distinct phases.

Today, many projects involve team members in multiple locations; this virtual team has to communicate as effectively as the single-location team of the past. Projects also include individuals from many different departments or segments. This cross-functional team is challenging because of different priorities, departmental points of view, and timing problems. Finally, managers face special problems when organizing projects that are global in nature. A multicultural team will present many challenges that projects managers have to contend with, not limited to time zones and language barriers, and including cultural differences and methods of communicating.

4. *Outsourced suppliers and vendors as team requirements.* The trend today is to outsource much of the work that in the past was kept internal and hands-on. As a result, much of the team activity you will lead will occur outside your physical location. Managing external team vendors or addressing the concerns of outside stakeholders presents new challenges to the modern project manager.

While project managers are concerned with control over schedules and budgets, as well as with interactions with team members, the evolving nature of today's organization presents many new efficient but challenging methods for doing business on all levels. A successful project manager has to be aware of these changing circumstances.

The Successful Project Manager

The successful project manager knows how to bring together the definition and control elements and operate them efficiently. The coordination of these two elements demands your leadership skills as well as organizational abilities.

In other words, as a qualified department manager, you already possess the attributes needed to succeed as a project manager as well. Chances are good that you will be selected to head up a project team based not only on the applicability of the project to your department, but also on your qualifications for the job. These qualifications are summarized in Figure 1-4 and elaborated on here:

1. *Organizational and leadership experience.* An executive seeking a qualified project manager naturally seeks an individual with a track record demonstrating basic organizational and leadership ability. These skills include the ability to:

▪ Manage the costs and expenses of the project

▪ Develop and monitor a schedule

▪ Lead a team well (i.e., by providing a required level of training and supervision when needed)

Figure 1-4. Project management qualifications.

1. Organizational and leadership experience.

2. Contact with needed resources.

3. Ability to coordinate a diverse resources pool.

4. Communication and procedural skills.

5. Ability to delegate and monitor work.

6. Dependability.

American Management Association
www.amanet.org

- Communicate well with outside resources as well as with top management

- Defuse any conflicts that arise, whether related to the work of the project or between individuals

2. *Contact with needed resources.* For projects involving a volume of coordination among departments, divisions, or subsidiaries, management seeks project managers who already maintain contact with those outside of their immediate department. Some refer to this skill as "integration management," but in fact it is nothing more than being able to work with many different resources at the same time and in an effective way that leads to results. The manager who has demonstrated the ability to work well with those outside of the department is also suited to run a project across departmental lines.

3. *Ability to coordinate a diverse resource pool.* By itself, contact outside of your department may not be enough. Effective project management requires the ability to work and communicate with personnel in other departments, even when their backgrounds, disciplines, and emphases are dissimilar. For example, different types of departments may have particular points of view concerning the importance of financial information, meeting deadlines, or working on a team that crosses departmental lines. Therefore, as project manager, you'll be required to balance all perspectives and find common ground.

4. *Communication and procedural skills.* Project managers have to receive and convey information to and from all team members while remembering that not everyone has the same background. There is a tendency for individuals in one department to share a point of view; however, project managers have to be able to work with everyone on the team and to respect the differences that people bring to the task. Understanding the scope of a project is a first step. You also need to be able to convey the information to your core team. For example, a marketing manager who can communicate well with an accounting department employee concerning the financial aspects of a project will be more likely to succeed than a manager who is not able to cross those communication lines. That manager also needs to be able to convey those same aspects and their importance to members of the team.

5. *Ability to delegate and monitor work.* Delegation by itself is not enough; you also need to ensure that:

- You delegate the work to a qualified person.

- The person you delegate to understands the assignment.

- Adequate oversight and supervision is available, if needed.

- The task is completed within budget and on schedule.

Managing time is critical for staying on schedule on two levels. You not only need to use your own time well and delegate when needed, but you also need to make sure that all individuals and subgroups of your team are working efficiently and effectively and staying on schedule. For example, a contractor building a house has to understand the processes involved in the work performed by each subcontractor, even when that work is specialized. The same is true for the project manager. If you delegate and then walk away, you have done only half the job. Delegation and monitoring have to work hand in hand, or they do not work at all.

6. *Dependability.* Management tests your dependability in only one way: by giving you responsibility and seeing whether you come through. Once management knows that you are able to take a project, define it, control the entire process, and deliver results, you gain the reputation for dependability. This is not limited to meeting the deadline and staying within budget; as project manager, you are also expected to set standards for quality and to meet them, as demonstrated in the final results.

These project management qualifications read like a list of evaluation points for every department manager. If you think of the aspects involved in running your department as a project of its own, then you already understand what is involved in organizing a project—the difference, of course, being that the project is finite in time, whereas your department's tasks are ongoing. Thus, every project manager is already qualified to take on a project, provided that it is related to the manager's skills, resources, and experience.

The Methodical Manager

The word *methodical* often refers to someone who is overly organized versus someone else who is more creative. However, you can be methodical and creative at the same time. A methodical approach to project management ensures consistent monitoring and adds to your chances of success.

True creativity requires discipline. A methodical, organized approach to problems ensures structure. Even when an outcome appears to be unstructured, it may well be the result of careful organization and planning. As project manager, you may need to take a creative approach to problem solving, especially considering that you may encounter problems not seen before. In this instance, the more methodically you approach the problem—that is, the more structured you are in your method of operation—the better your chances for finding creative and appropriate solutions.

The methodical manager knows the right questions to ask. When projects are assigned, your checklist should include the seven questions listed in Figure 1-5. Each is explained as follows:

1. *What is the purpose of the project?* From the description of your assignment, you make a series of assumptions about what is expected. But in fact, the person giving you the assignment could have something entirely different in mind. A large number of communication problems are derived from misunderstandings about definition.

2. *What will the outcome look like?* Be sure you know precisely what you are expected to produce at the end of the project. If you are asked to write procedures, clarify whether you are expected to produce a manual for the entire company or just provide each department with guidelines. When a project requires a written report, how much detail

Figure 1-5. A checklist of questions to ask.

1. What is the purpose of this project?

2. What will the outcome look like?

3. What problems will be encountered and solved?

4. What is my responsibility?

5. What is my authority?

6. What is my budget?

7. What is my deadline?

should be included? Will you be expected to make a presentation and, if so, in what forum?

3. *What problems will be encountered and solved?* Always assume that a project should be designed to identify and solve a number of well-defined problems. You cannot expect to be provided with a complete list of problems; in fact, the project process itself will invariably include a degree of discovery.

Even when you expect to encounter a range of problems beyond those mentioned in the initial assignment, a project should begin with an assumption: A specific series of problems will be identified, and your purpose is to solve them or suggest alternatives. Define your project in those terms.

4. *What is my responsibility?* As project manager, you deserve a clear definition of what you will be expected to do. Will you be responsible for identifying and recommending solutions, for putting them into effect, or only for comparing possible alternatives?

Be sure you understand exactly what level of responsibility you are being given. In some cases, you may be given responsibility to put changes into effect, but only in one division, subsidiary, or department.

5. *What is my authority?* The question of authority is perhaps of greater importance than that of responsibility. One without the other is useless. If you need to recruit team members from other departments, change procedures, or implement a final decision related to your project, that level of authority should be explained clearly—not only to you, but to other managers whose departments will be affected.

6. *What is my budget?* Some projects can be executed with little expense beyond the commitment of time. Others may involve spending months conducting research, writing reports, or purchasing equipment, all of which takes up staff time as well.

Always begin the project with a clear understanding of the budget. Don't overlook the expense of staff time, since that has to be included in the total project cost required to achieve the project's desired result. In practice, projects often are assigned within one department and you are expected to execute the project without an additional budget while also continuing to perform your normal routines. Is this realistic? By clearly defining the scope of the project, you might discover that additional budgeting will be required. This has to be communicated upward to senior management so that you will be able to proceed with the resources you require.

7. *What is the deadline?* Always ask for a specific deadline. Only when you know the result that's expected can you establish a schedule and plan for execution of the project's phases. It often occurs that a deadline is unrealistic. If you believe you have not been provided with enough time, you need to take one of two steps. First, ask for more time, explaining why the original deadline is not practical. Or second, ask for an increased budget to hire more staff and accelerate the project's schedule.

In scheduling your project, it may be possible to overlap some phases and cut the time requirements to a degree. It is more desirable to build buffers into your phases so that schedule overruns can be absorbed without missing the final deadline. However, you are more likely to find yourself working against time without any flexibility.

Project Classification

The method you employ in planning and organizing your project depends on the type of project. If your department's routines are more like projects than recurring tasks, then you will be more accustomed to facing new problems from day to day.

While the steps involved in defining, controlling, and finalizing a project may be the same, the effort is going to vary based on the project. Compare the different emphases for these projects:

Project scenario 1: Test marketing a new product. The method of market testing is well understood within the department, so project emphasis is concentrated in two areas: selecting a representative test region and evaluating results accurately.

Project scenario 2: Installing an automated system. In this project, the definition phase requires great care and effort. You may need to decide exactly which automation requirements are needed and which are not. The project may need to be modified to prioritize routines to be automated first, followed by those less suitable for automation or those that are excludable altogether. The scheduling of this project should also allow for transition issues, such as resistance to change among departments, the need for training and conversion time, and potential software problems that will have to be corrected during the project's final phases.

Project scenario 3: Changing departmental procedures. You may have more than the usual amount of flexibility in the deadline for this project. However, a realistic schedule should allow for time to speak with each employee. Changing procedures requires that each process be incorporated into the new system if it is to work well. The complexity of this project rests with how well your project team is able to document actual work requirements and incorporate those needs into the new procedure.

From these examples, it is obvious that every project has its own special problems. These may relate to schedule, budget, or the problems associated with working across departmental lines. Every project can be classified according to its scope and complexity based on:

- Resources you have to employ outside of your department

- The size of your project team

■ The time span between inception and deadline

■ Your familiarity with the information

. . . .

As project manager, you must be able to stay on schedule and within budget and meet your final deadline—but all of that demands careful planning and organization. Subsequent chapters in this book explain how to put methods to work for mastering even the most complex project. No job is too large if it is first defined completely and then broken down into logical and progressive steps. Chapter 2 explains the initial phase: creating the plan and defining objectives.

══ WORK PROJECT ══

1. Explain the distinction between projects and routines according to the following criteria:
   a. Range of functions
   b. Relationship of activities or routines
   c. Goals and deadlines
   d. Project results

2. Name the three constraints under which a project is executed. Explain how these constraints define your control responsibility.

3. Compare the definition and control elements of a project. Why are both essential to the successful execution of the assignment?

2

The Six Sigma Approach

*What is a committee? A group
Of the unwilling, picked from
The unfit, to do the unnecessary.*

—RICHARD HARKNESS—

"That was a tough budget meeting, the worst I've ever seen," one supervisor told another. "They cut *everything*."

"Everything?"

"Yes, and I mean everything. They even cut back on the Six Sigma program. Now it's known as Four Sigma."

The popular view of committees as inefficient groups prevails in all organizations, even in those depending on the consensus approach to projects, quality control, and even simple decision making. However, a committee does not have to be inefficient. By definition, a project team is a committee, but it is expected to produce results. This means that the project management team needs a system in place to make it form effectively, unlike the traditional committee, and to achieve the desired results. This is where Six Sigma plays a role.

The Six Sigma system is an approach to quality control that has become popular in most of the Fortune 500 companies, military organizations, and throughout the American corporate world. This is so because Six Sigma produces results on two levels. Most apparent are its structure and definition. Less apparently, however, is its cultural aspect. The Six Sigma approach relies on a complete change in organizational thinking. Rather than continuing to operate on the theory that "It's not my job," under the Six Sigma organizational culture, everyone is involved in quality and excellence.

Putting aside the cynicism that managers often adopt when confronted with one of many varieties of a quality control system, Six Sigma is quite different. It certainly has roots in quality control and manufacturing, but, applied universally to organizational systems, it is much more. For a project manager, Six Sigma provides a method for defining a project, tracking it, and enabling all members of the team to excel and to succeed in executing a project, whether aimed at quality control, changes in internal systems, or greater working efficiency.

The Meaning of Six Sigma

The Greek letter sigma (σ) is used to denote the statistical standard deviation, or a rate of defects in any process. The sigma formula is complex, but it has real significance in identifying how well a process works and, of equal value, how well an improved program works to change the rate of defects (known as "standard deviation," "spread," or "variability" to statisticians).

When standard deviation is taken up to six levels, the result is 3.4 defects per million, or as close to perfection as you can expect statisti-

Valuable Resource

To calculate standard deviation, use the free online calculator at http://www.easycalculation.com/statistics/standard-deviation.php

cally. The outcome of 99.9997 percent easily rounds up to 100 percent. So Six Sigma is defined as the ultimate perfection. No process is expected to change to ensure a 100 percent outcome. But the philosophy of Six Sigma states that by knowing what perfection looks like, it becomes possible to measure improvement. Following are the various Sigma levels in terms of defects per million and the representative percentages that apply:

Sigma Level	Defects per Million	Percentage (%)
6.0	3.4	99.9997
5.0	233.0	99.977
4.0	6,210.0	99.379
3.0	66,807.0	93.32
2.0	308,538.0	69.1
1.0	691,462.0	30.9

There are significant differences between degrees of Sigma. So in measuring improvements in terms of defect-free processes, changing from a 2 Sigma to a 3 Sigma is a vast improvement. This is a central theme in the six Sigma concept: It is intended as a method for measuring outcomes in a tangible and specific manner.

So when any operations are performed, you can measure the Sigma of outcomes. Before your project, for example, you might observe that out of 1,415 identified operations, 209 fell outside the acceptable range of outcomes. (This may refer to product defects, faulty repair operations, negative customer contacts, late deliveries, financial results containing errors, or any process that can be measured.) This means that 1,206 operations resulted in the acceptable range of outcomes. In Six Sigma, this is quantified as $1,206 \div 1,415 = 85.2$ percent. This is slightly better than a 2.5 Sigma. If a project could improve the acceptable outcomes to 1,325 (meaning reducing unacceptables to 90), it would improve to a level of over 3.0 Sigma: $1{,}325 \div 1{,}415 = 93.6$ percent.

This approach to quality control is the perfect venue for project management. In so many instances, project managers face the dilemma of not knowing how to measure results. If the project is simply designed to cut expenses or speed up processes, outcome is easily quantified without Six Sigma. But so many projects are not as clearly defined that a starting point in a project may be to add that definition to the process. This gives the manager and the project team a scorekeeping procedure, so that everyone will know whether they are on schedule, within budget, and accomplishing their clearly stated project goals. It is immediately apparent that applying Six Sigma in the project definition adds great value to all phases of the project.

The origins of Six Sigma are traced back to the 1980s, when Motorola initiated the concept. A Motorola engineer named Mikel Harry realized that internal systems lacked a means for measuring even when improvement initiatives were put in place. Harry argued that by changing project systems so that variations could be measured, it would provide a means for identifying improvements as well. Other quality systems measure only performance; Harry designed Six Sigma to track variation (defects) in processes and to develop methods for reducing those variations.

By the 1990s the concept had been formulated, tested, and expanded, and many corporations adopted it as both a project management system and an organizational culture. Six Sigma teams are not based on rank within the corporation, in which executives oversee managers, and so forth down the line to the rank and file. Instead, a team leader and a team are set up based on qualifications to execute a project, crossing both rank and departmental lines. In many respects, this approach was revolutionary. It took form under the leadership of Jack Welch at General Electric (GE). Welch demonstrated that Six Sigma was much more than just another name for a quality-control initiative. By 1999, GE's cost savings exceeded $1 billion.

The projects GE ran were measured in terms of cost reduction, a natural way to create performance tests in any corporation. However, GE also experienced improvements in production, communications, and supply chain processes, all contributing to the impressive annual savings that Welch attributed to the company's Six Sigma program.

Business Process Management (BPM)

A Six Sigma approach to project management begins, like all well-run projects, with specific definitions. Business Process Management (BCM), which has also been called the Business Process Model, describes how work moves from step to step through the organization. The same model is effectively applied to describe a more focused project, so that the project team can define those processes and identify the important focus areas (weak links in the process, likely points where defects occur, or bottleneck areas within the process itself).

BPM is the basis for the visual representation of a process. The well-known flowchart is intended to break down a process into its specific steps, to identify the person, department, or team responsible for execution, and to delineate the all-important flow (where a step originates, what gets done, and where it goes next). Computer people are used to seeing processes graphically represented in a top-to-bottom format. For work flow, it makes more sense for the flow to be shown going from left to right, with the responsibility represented by levels and easily viewed and with the timeline identified along the way. This left-to-right concept makes it easy to identify all of the elements, including multiple processes that invariably come into play. It would be rare for a process to involve a single process line; it is far more likely that two or more concurrent steps are going to be undertaken. While this accelerates the possibility of error or defect, it is a reality.

Figure 2–1 shows a simplified version of the horizontal flowchart. This concept is explored in greater depth in Chapters 7, 8, and 9. In this illustration, four separate departments, teams, or individuals are involved. These are represented on the horizontal plane in the illustration. Because the execution of each step is managed by different levels (people or groups), they are referred to as *areas of responsibility*. You can also see in this simplified flowchart how a process may split into several parts. As the process moves from left to right, the interaction between areas of responsibility and the time involved is also easily ob-

Figure 2-1. Horizontal flowchart.

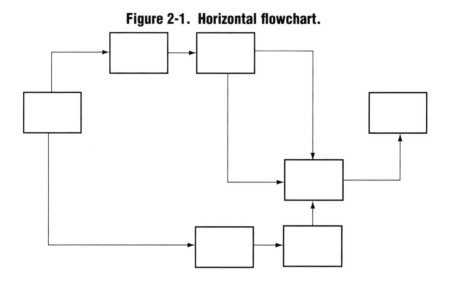

served. If each segment of the process is identified in terms of time (days or weeks required for completion), the BPM can also be relied on to identify timing of the entire project. Steps requiring more time are represented with greater space between steps.

BPM is more than a passive summary of work flow. It can and should serve as the basic outline of the whole project, allowing you to observe the areas of responsibility, time involved, multiple process flow, potential timing bottlenecks, and weak links. A so-called weak link is most likely to occur whenever the process passes from one area of responsibility to another.

The BPM approach, as a starting point in the Six Sigma approach to project management, defines all of the steps in the project, so that you can ensure that nothing has been overlooked or ignored. When you begin to analyze processes in terms of BMP flow, any omissions become apparent very quickly. You can further emphasize likely weak links by adding emphasis to the horizontal flowchart. For example, in Figure 2–2, black rectangles are used to highlight. Here, six specific places are identified where weak links occur, also meaning where defects or errors are most likely. These occur at any place on the BPM where the process moves from one area of responsibility to another.

Once you have focused on these handoff points, you will be able

Figure 2-2. Horizontal flowchart with weak link emphasis added.

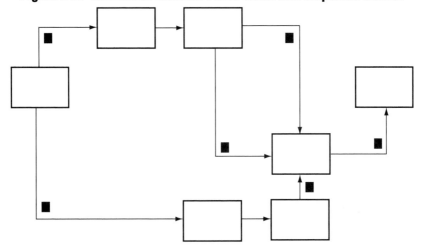

to reduce the problems in any project by a significant degree. This is due to the tendency for problems to arise at those very points. It is true that weak links also arise even when processes are being executed within an area of responsibility, but the more serious weak links are far more likely in the places shown in the illustration.

Project Participants and Goal Definitions

In the Six Sigma approach to project management, a series of individual participants is involved. It is crucial to make distinctions among these individuals. Projects often fall apart due to lack of clarity about who is the actual leader, who is on the team, what each member's duties are, and who benefits from the process.

Six Sigma is quite elaborate and formal in its structure and design, and a team consists of numerous individuals. Some of these include a leadership team or council, sponsor, implementation director, coach, team leader, team member, and process owner. For many projects and teams, this formality involves excessive layers. In a formal and complex project, that level of organization might be necessary, and in that case the project team should be structured along very specific Six Sigma lines. Although this degree of formality is instructive, an assumption is made here that fewer participation layers are adequate in a majority of cases. Projects often are short term, confined to one department or segment, and with a very limited number of people on the team. With this in mind, a few participants are identified, including:

1. *Project manager.* The manager, or team leader, should be one individual, clearly identified from the onset and given adequate authority to lead the team through the project. As a project manager, you define the ultimate goal in consultation with your team, set a schedule and budget, assign specific tasks, and ensure that the project goals are met.

2. *Project team members.* Team members may come from different departments and may even outrank the project manager in the organizational hierarchy. Each team member is assumed to be chosen by the manager due to a set of skills and knowledge essential for completion of the project. This also defines what each member will do within the team, and how each member works with other team members.

3. *Process owner.* In Six Sigma, the process owner is identified as the individual or department that benefits from an improved process or system or who will be responsible for executing a series of tasks in a newly defined process. This is an interesting concept often overlooked in the non–Six Sigma project management system. But it is an essential element. Process owners are often also project managers or team members, but not always. An assumption may be added to the project management concept, however, to make it work better: Being aware of the identity of a process owner largely defines how a project is defined and structured, as well as how it is organized and executed.

The identification of a project manager, team members, and process owner also shape the goals of the project. The expression, "If you don't know where you're going, any road will get you there" has application in project management. Defining the elements of the project has to start with identifying the essential people who will design and execute it. Goal setting is a definition phase that has to be completed before anything else can occur. Otherwise, the project team will find itself on "any road" without a clear objective and without the ability to know whether it is moving in the right direction.

It is very useful in defining the goals of a project to move beyond the obvious and common ideal of cutting expenses or speeding up processing time. The financial goal is important within the organization, but more may be involved. Goals such as improved safety, security, internal controls, lower rate of defects, improved customer satisfaction and response, risk mitigation and planning, and any number of additional goals can and should play a role in defining the project.

A second element in goal setting should always involve customer service. A popular belief is that employees either interact with customers or they do not. So a marketing and sales orientation identifies end user customers or clients (buyers) as the most important contact, whereas nonmarketing and nonsales employees have no contact with customers. So mailroom employees, shipping and receiving personnel, accountants, analysts, internal auditors, administrative assistants, and even top executives are set apart and viewed as belonging to the group of employees who never see a customer.

An enlightened variation of this organizational culture is to assume that everyone has a customer. Some customers, such as those known to sales and marketing, are external. Others are internal. Anyone who receives or sends mail is a customer of the mailroom, anyone getting a paycheck is a customer of the payroll department, and anyone requiring clerical help is a customer of a variety of administrative assistants, clerks, and other office employees. In other words, *everyone* has a customer, and *everyone* is in the customer service business.

This enlightened view of organizational culture, promoted by the Six Sigma philosophy, helps to broaden the project management concept as well. It helps to explain how and why one goal of every project should be to improve "customer service" in its many different definitions. Every project, no matter what its design or purpose, contains customer service elements under this universal definition. The inclusion of all employees and departments, as providers and customers, also clarifies all of the project goals, as well as improving overall performance and interaction.

Defining Goals in Terms of Customer Service

A project's initial stated goal is likely to be fairly simple. For example:

- Reduce costs in the department to meet the current budget and produce greater profit margins in future years.

- Identify causes of defects and reduce the defect rate.

- Improve response time to customer complaints.

These typical goals relate to the most immediate problem, and project teams often are formed with these initial problems in mind. The problem and solution may seem quite evident. But upon examination, the problems might be more complex, requiring more effective solutions. For example:

- Reducing costs in the department might require vastly improved internal controls to reduce idle time, theft, or inefficiency; these require not only improved internal controls but more effective use of human resources and improved monitoring.

- Causes of defects might include outdated equipment, poor training, or employee morale problems, so that improved processes alone will not address the underlying issues; the causes may be more complex than simply pinning outcomes to a desired goal.

- Response time to complaints most often includes poor communication between complaint sources and responsible individuals or departments, or improvement may demand higher levels of training or even revisiting the basic production or delivery of products; the goal of speeding up response time is only an attribute of a larger problem.

The Six Sigma approach to project management looks at goals in terms of underlying causes, and these drive the process (BPM). If it is driven by the desired results, many projects are not going to be permanent or effective. Keeping the customer (external or internal) in mind, the effective design of a project has to rely on defining these root causes as part of developing solutions.

Another valuable concept within Six Sigma is called Voice of the Customer (VOC), which refers to an overlay of customer requirements as part of defining the project and its goals. Project managers who employ VOC in the defining phase of a plan continually ask themselves and their team, "What are the customer's expectations and desires?" (Remember, the end user may be external or internal.) In many instances, the internal customer is also the process owner, but not always. When a project is aimed at improving a working environment or process for a specific department, for example, then that department is both customer and process owner. When a project is designed to improve quality, efficiency, or response to an external customer, then the process owner will be the department, sector, or employee responsible for communication with that external customer. So VOC may be a direct link to an external consumer or a set of expectations on the part of an internal customer (process owner).

Paying attention to VOC, with a clear focus on the desired end result, is the goal for every project manager. The action plan expressed in a Six Sigma program is naturally well suited to every project; it is called DMAIC (define, measure, analyze, improve, control). This five-part study of quality as part of the project helps to deliver an excellent and successful result. It formalizes the process every project manager needs to move through. One drawback to Six Sigma is its formality and use of many abbreviations for multipart processes. These highly structured approaches to project management vary in applicability. The structure is not necessary for smaller projects, but it serves as a useful guideline for how to begin:

1. *Define.* In this first phase, you need to identify the crucial components of the team and study the proposed outcome from the point of view of the process owner and of any and all stakeholders. (A *stakeholder*, in Six Sigma terms, is anyone with a direct interest in the project and its outcome.) You also need to express a project goal. In Six Sigma, this is called the *project charter*, used to summarize the business case, scope, and goals of the project. Finally, you need to begin filling in a process map, the elements of the project including suppliers, steps,

and output. Six Sigma calls this the SIPOC (suppliers, input, process, output, and customers). Without definition, the project cannot take shape or reach its goal. The steps in the defining process are the foundation of the project, an essential starting point on which everything else is going to be built.

2. *Measure.* In this phase, three specific steps are involved. First and most obvious is data collection, the activity of deciding what data will be required and then actually accumulating it, possibly from a variety of areas. All sources (input, process, output) can be used for the data that the project team will need. Second is data evaluation. To understand how a process is currently working and what is needed to make improvements, your project team will have to evaluate data, observe the rate and likelihood of defects, focus on weak links, and quantify the defect rate to decide how to reduce it. The third step is the development of systems and processes aimed at preventing defects before they occur. Six Sigma folks call this the Failure Mode and Effects Analysis (FMEA), the process of determining precisely what can go wrong and how to reduce problems. The risk management aspects of this process are crucial, even when you do not use the technical terminology for it. The risk management process may include rating possible defects or failures by (a) the potential of occurrence, (b) the ability to detect the defect, and (c) a level of severity. This risk management rating system helps in determining how best to proceed in ranking and then reducing defects.

3. *Analyze.* In this self-monitoring phase, a project team decides how effectively it is progressing through the project and whether its changes are effective. This should be as complex as required or as simple as necessary to be effective. The purpose is to be able to identify and rank defects *and* then to conclude whether specific changes and controls are effective. The analysis includes a study of root causes, processes, data, resources, and communications. Any or all of these may contribute to failures and often define and point to weak links.

For example, if source data are flawed, then the entire process starts out at a disadvantage and will be more failure-prone. If processes lack controls, then failures are inherently more frequent. The data are assumed to be reliable in a controlled process, but if variables are present then weak links are inevitable. Resources (notably human resources) must be adequate to the task, so equipment must be effective and in working order, and employees have to be completely trained to keep defects or failures to a minimum. Finally, communications are essential for process control. It was a revolutionary idea a few years ago when Toyota instituted a system allowing any auto assembly worker to stop the entire line if he or she saw a defect. Yet it makes perfect sense: Stopping the problem right away prevents further problems. Although Toyota had to overcome a cultural resistance among employees monitoring one another, the ability to effectively communicate cut defects considerably.

4. *Improve.* Measuring and analyzing are essential steps, but they are only valuable when you take additional steps to improve current conditions. As project manager, your responsibility is not limited to getting the steps completed. If known defects or weak links are not fixed, the project will not be successful. This is where the project team becomes valuable. Team members may be encouraged to offer alternative solutions to discovered weak links or failures. If many good ideas come forward, part of the project dynamic may include experimenting with different solutions.

Part of the improve phase often overlooked is the development of plans for future changes. Today, most organizations are continually handling new technology, delivery systems, markets, and, of course, threats. Risk management requires that today's solutions be flexible enough to adjust as future threats emerge or as today's processing environment evolves. Once you identify the weak links in a process, you will also know where to plan for renovations of a newly installed system of controls and counter measures.

5. *Control.* This is the last phase. To many organizational leaders, the word "control" simply means checking and verifying. The idea here is to make sure that all steps are taken and that any security threats are countered and removed, as applied to anything from balancing a worksheet to safeguarding inventory. But this is only part of the control universe. Quality control, development, and enforcement of standards, including reduction of defects as the most apparent version, is what Six Sigma is all about, at least initially. Every project manager will be concerned with quality control in all aspects of the work. However, control also relies on standardization. Processes are made more reliable when each step is made as uniform as possible. Value chain analysis has shown that the exceptions slow down processes, add costs, and may also lead to additional defects and failures. A standardized process reduces the problems.

Another aspect of control is development of an appropriate response. This has to be built into the entire procedure. For example, if Toyota had merely trained its assembly line employees on how to recognize defects and communicate them in a written report, the final product would have gone forward without being fixed. The system was made effective by allowing anyone on the line to pull a cord and stop everything right away. This was an appropriate response. It had the added benefit of improving a sense of teamwork among the entire crew, but, from a control point of view, it was crucial to stop the line *immediately* when a defect was recognized.

The response to discovered defects is part of your project management challenge. Whether you adhere to a strict and complex interpretation of Six Sigma or merely apply its principles informally, a project is not complete until you make specific recommendations to fix them. Some projects are passive in nature, limited to a study of the current process, but lacking authority to make changes. So a project manager may issue a report describing the flaws and providing recommendations to management. But what if no action is taken?

If you are given the job of project manager but not the authority to put changes into effect, this can be a frustrating exercise, especially if management merely files your report and nothing changes. That is a waste of resources and a misuse of your talents as well as those of your team. To make sure that Six Sigma and other systematic approaches work, remember to add value by including the following attributes to your final report:

1. First and foremost, analyze the cost savings your proposed changes offer, and lay these out on page one.

2. Propose very specific action plans that can be taken immediately. Outline them and explain how they improve the situation.

3. Unless some other department or sector is responsible for the process, volunteer to execute the changes as part of your project.

4. If you will not be given the responsibility for executing improvements, anticipate who will be given the task and recommend a step-by-step action plan.

Six Sigma is an incredible tool for managing complex projects, and it works exceptionally well in large organizations with expanded bureaucracies. However, the formality is not always appropriate. For any project limited to a single department or sector within the company, a simplified approach, using the same defining aspects of Six Sigma but without the tiers and operational rules, may be more effective. This is also true when a project team is limited in number. Some large complex projects require coordination among many departments and sectors, and in those instances Six Sigma's structure is valuable both in training and execution. A good guideline is simply that the complexity of the project's team structure should be justified by its scope and requirements, and the structure should never be more complex or more formal than circumstances demand.

WORK PROJECT

1. Describe the major aspects of the Six Sigma program in relation to its quality-control features and as part of the organizational culture.

2. Give three examples of a weak link in a system, and describe conditions within the process where these are most likely to occur.

3. Provide an example of each step in the DMAIC process, applied to a typical project that you might be asked to lead.

Creating the Plan

Beyond the loathing and the fear lies one of the best-kept secrets in American business. "Planning," it turns out, is really no more—and no less—than another word for good management.

—BRUCE G. POSNER—

"Planning is the key," the project manager explained to her assistant as their lunch came to an end. "I invited you here today to emphasize that point. As part of this team, I expect you to understand the importance of planning ahead."

She stopped as the waiter approached and accepted the tab. She looked at the total for a moment, then whispered to her assistant, "Can you lend me twenty dollars?"

All successful projects begin with a clear definition of the end result. You need to identify the purpose and structure of the job, what the outcome will look like upon completion, the problems that will be solved, and the objectives you need to meet in your capacity of project manager. Before you actually begin work on any project, be sure that you ask these questions:

■ ***Exactly what objectives am I expected to meet?*** Has the project been defined well enough so that you understand your assignment?

If not, you need to ask for clarification. By identifying objectives, you will be able to define the proper end result.

■ ***Who is the project for?*** Another way to define the end result is by making sure you know who will use the project results, and for what purpose. Does an executive want the information in order to make a more informed decision? Or is the report going to be published for all to see? In other words, who is the audience?

■ ***What problems will be solved by the end result?*** Coming up with a new procedure, identifying the feasibility of an idea, or arriving at conclusions about the market's response to a new product; all are end results of projects. However, to ensure that the end result is worthwhile, you also need to know what problems are to be solved by the effort you put into the project.

Setting Leadership Goals

After you arrive at a clear definition, schedule, and budget for your project, you need to plan for leading your project team. Because team members often view projects as intrusions into their normal routines, or extra work imposed on them, you may have to contend with resistance within the team, or at the very least assist team members in resolving scheduling conflicts.

To make a project work smoothly, you may also need to alter your

Other Resources

Project management planning contains many aspects—from configuration management and problem tracking systems to asset management training, consulting, and career advancement issues—that are beyond the scope of this book. For an interesting online exercise including free advice and consultation, check the Massachusetts Institute of Technology (MIT) website www.mit.edu/ist/pmm/. Although the methodology on this site is directed at specific projects, its toolkit and requirements sections are very useful to any project manager.

leadership style. Define your functions clearly along with the specific functions of the team. Some suggestions are listed in Figure 3-1 and expanded on here:

1. *Clarify your leadership role.* While department managers develop their leadership style over time, the project manager does not have the same luxury. As a project manager, you often are thrust into the role on a temporary basis, often having to lead individuals who do not report to you in normal circumstances. Even employees reporting to you will be operating in a different environment as part of the project team. Thus, it is essential that you let your project team know how you perceive your role as team leader.

Your stance should be altered to suit the complexity of the project, the time it will take, and the size and personalities of your team. Most projects will require you to act not so much as supervisor, but more as a coordinator. Your primary function will involve oversight, or working to ensure that resources work together, schedules are followed, budgets are controlled, and the end result is kept firmly in mind. As a department manager, you may perform daily routines along with employees; as project manager, your role probably will not allow for as much direct participation in the execution of tasks.

Figure 3-1. Project leadership goals.

1. Clarify your leadership role.

2. Follow through on all aspects of the job.

3. Emphasize organization and scheduling.

4. Be aware of team priorities and conflicts.

5. Be available to team members.

6. Ask for participation and respond to it.

7. Always remember the end result.

2. *Follow through on all aspects of the job.* Remember that because projects are exceptions, team members won't understand their roles as well as you would like. Most employees are going to approach their tasks with a point of view developed in the department, where permanent assignments are typical. You may need to work closely with some team members to ensure that they understand what they are expected to do. Your emphasis should be on the fact that the routines performed are temporary in nature. Some individuals will have difficulty understanding the perspective, so your job is to educate and train.

3. *Emphasize organization and scheduling.* You will depend on exceptional organization and strict adherence to a schedule in order to meet your deadline. Thus, the division of assignments to team members has to be thought through carefully. It may help to write down everything and to develop checklists to ensure that work progresses as expected, everyone knows what their role is in the bigger picture, and each phase is finished on time. Also keep a checklist for yourself of problems that arise as you progress through the job. Attack problems immediately and resolve them to ensure that you will be able to finish one phase and get the next one going.

4. *Be aware of team priorities and conflicts.* On a practical level, your team members need to continue performing their regular routines in addition to working on your project. That means they face deadlines and crunch times in their departmental cycles, and during those times your project will take a low priority. This situation is augmented when team members report to you for the project and to someone else in their departmental routines.

Talk to each team member and identify how their work cycles progress. Arrange your own schedule to allow for their routine demands. If necessary, reassign tasks or provide double coverage for ongoing project demands so that work doesn't have to stop for a week at a time. Also, stay in touch with each team member's supervisor to help avoid priority conflicts.

5. *Be available to team members.* As an effective project manager, you need to provide team members with the support they need.

This means that you are the problem solver on the team. You need to make yourself available to help team members work through problems, including project-related difficulties as well as scheduling conflicts.

6. *Ask for participation and respond to it.* A project team should function more efficiently than a department in at least one important respect: The project requires true teamwork, whereas the department is characterized by a well-established relationship between a leader and followers. Using the model of the organizational chart, a department tends to work vertically, whereas a project team tends to function more horizontally. You are the project leader, but the team attribute is emphasized more. Thus, the level of participation by team members also tends to be different. Ask your team to offer ideas and solutions, to explore alternatives that can make the project more successful. Be willing to change your procedures when a team member comes up with a better idea.

7. *Always remember the end result.* Project managers can lose sight of the desired end result when they are busy solving schedule and budget problems, working through team members' conflicts, and trying to balance their own recurring duties with those of the project. You will need to remind yourself constantly what you are trying to achieve in the project and how your decisions need to be aimed at that end result.

Building Your Resource Network

Project managers plan effectively by identifying and then building a network. This network consists of people from their department, other departments, and in some cases, outside of the company.

Having the right people on your project team is essential for the success of the project, whether their role is active or advisory. You will coordinate and execute your project with a combination of a fairly small core team and an extensive advisory network. This keeps down costs and maximizes efficiency. The bigger the team, the more difficult it will be to keep things organized, so the small core team can help to streamline the entire process.

Example 1

A sales department manager was assigned the project of developing procedures for the sales force for following up with customers. Salespeople had not been delivering orders correctly and in some cases did not supply all of the information necessary for order fulfillment. This situation led to a higher than acceptable level of returns and numerous customer complaints. The sales manager was asked to revamp procedures, rewrite a manual, and design a new order form that would ensure that the fulfillment department would be able to correctly deliver the goods.

The project manager wrote up a list of the people who could help meet the project objectives. They included:

■ *Salespeople Familiar With the Order Completion Process and Its Problems.* Their participation would include suggestions on how to improve the entire process, most notably in the design of an improved order form. In addition, these employees would be valuable in suggesting ways to improve their follow-up procedures with customers.

■ *The Manager of the Fulfillment Department.* This individual was aware of the same problems, but from the other side. This manager would provide the project manager with information about how to help the fulfillment side to work more efficiently, including suggestions for form design and improved communication between the sales and fulfillment departments.

■ *A Customer Service Employee.* This employee from the customer service department had recently completed a report summarizing the nature of complaints received from customers. This employee was aware of the errors reported by customers as well as the growing trend in complaints. The problems related to delays, shipment of the wrong products, incomplete orders, and lack of follow-up by the salesperson.

■ *Outside Supplier.* The supplier provided input on the design and printing of new forms.

In addition, the project manager assigned two employees from the sales department to help with the task of compiling information from other team members and designing preliminary forms, writing drafts of new procedures, and following up on suggestions from others. One of the most important functions of the project was to come up with one form and one procedure that would satisfy the requirements of three departments: sales, fulfillment, and customer service.

Example 2

A sales manager included two sales department employees on the project team, but also included advisory team members from the sales, fulfillment, and customer service departments. The "core" project team included the project manager and two sales employees; this group managed the majority of the work compiled from others and put in the greatest number of hours.

Structuring Your Project Team

In addition to separating out your core team and advisory team members, you also need to decide how to organize the structure of the project team. You may employ a direct report structure or an organizational structure. The best alternative depends on the nature of the project, the number of team members, and your personal preferences and management/delegation style.

A direct structure is one in which you, as project manager, are in direct contact with each and every team member, without a middle reporting layer. This alternative makes sense when your core team includes relatively few people and is similar to the organizational makeup of a small department. It is simple, involves a desirable element of direct contact, and lacks the bureaucracy that sometimes results when middle reporting layers are created. The direct team structure is illustrated in Figure 3-2.

The organizational structure becomes necessary when the complexity of your project requires a larger team, meaning that the control and monitoring functions take up most of your time. The larger, more

Figure 3-2. Direct team structure.

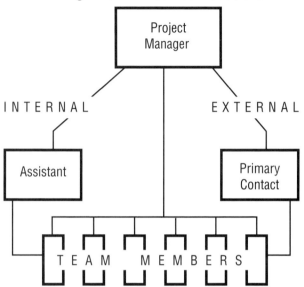

complex project demands a more formal reporting network, including at the very least an internal assistant to oversee the work of team members. You delegate supervisory responsibility to the assistant so that your own time can be used to control and oversee the project. To operate as an effective project manager, you should continue to keep in touch with all team members and avoid unnecessary bureaucracy. Remember, the project is temporary and has to operate efficiently; complex power structures will destroy the project completely. The purpose of the organizational structure is to share responsibility for a large group while effectively managing the budget and schedule. This structure is illustrated in Figure 3-3.

Example

You are responsible for two projects. The first is a short-term, fairly simple job involving three employees in your department. For this project, you are using the direct team structure. Your second project is far more complicated, both in its objective and the size of your team. You

Figure 3-3. Organizational team structure.

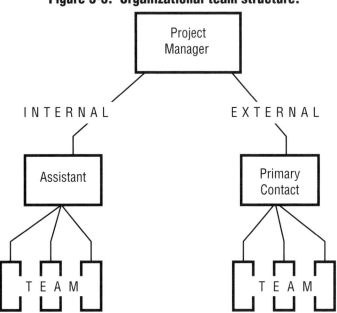

appoint an assistant to coordinate the work of the internal team members, and you also depend on a fellow manager who is the primary contact for outside resources (i.e., project team members in that manager's department). Your primary function is to ensure that the budget is not exceeded and that each phase is completed on time.

Defining the Project's Scope

Once your team is in place, an initial meeting to discuss the project's scope can be revealing. Even if you believe you have a thorough grasp of the project, you may be surprised to learn quite a lot from team members. This is likely to expand the project to include valuable benefits or processes you had not anticipated.

Broadly speaking, you need to make sure your team members understand exactly what the project is designed to accomplish. This is not always possible by project title alone. So a starting point is needed to explain why the project is being done, what problems it is intended to fix, and how improvements are going to work. This requires not only a clear definition of what needs to be done, but also of the desired outcome. As obvious as all this might seem, many plans are launched without this initial discussion among leaders and team members.

As a secondary point, it is essential to discuss how this project fits into the larger organizational puzzle. Many people, even including managers, have a myopic view of the organization and how their functions fit into it. For example, a mailroom employee might say that the business of the organization is to receive and send mail. An accountant may say the business of the organization is to document expenses and write checks, and a marketing employee sees the business as attracting a larger market. These are all aspects of the overall company, but invariably there is more to it. The discussion any group of organizational employees can have about this question is going to be enlightening, especially if your team includes people from different departments.

If the project crosses departmental or sector lines, the scope is going to be more complex than a project existing within departmental lines. Your actions have to consider territorial interests, schedules, and possibly even conflicts among supervisors and managers, some of whom may view a change in agenda as a direct threat. Who is impacted? How can you describe a project in terms of *benefits* rather than as imposed changes?

Finally, invite team members to talk about the stakeholders to the project. These are often much more complex than some people will assume. A stakeholder is not always limited to the people who generate input, process it, or receive the output. Every business operating unit affected by the process is also a stakeholder. If your project has a direct impact on sales and marketing, you need employees from those departments on your team, so that impacts on those departments and on customers will be monitored and considered. In other words, the assumption should not be limited only to those who are expected to do the work; it has to expand to include a range of departments and individuals affected by the work as well. In some very formalized projects, especially those operated as part of a Six Sigma venue, stakeholders are named to sit on a steering committee overseeing the project or assigned a position on the team. In some instances, oversight committees have to approve recommended changes. The scope of this close oversight is going to vary based on your mandate, the scope of the project, and management's philosophy about how closely project managers have to be monitored or how freely they are allowed to operate.

This initial discussion with your team should be at the core of your project announcement meeting, which can be thought of as the kickoff for the team itself. The tone set during this meeting relies on how willingly team members are participating, overall organizational morale, internal team building and training, and your own leadership style.

Holding a Project Announcement Meeting

Getting your project off to a healthy, well-defined start depends on your approach. How you lead, how you define work processes and goals, and how you organize your team all determine how the project will proceed. It is important as part of this preliminary step to communicate your purpose and your approach to the project team. Thus, the project announcement meeting is essential.

An initial gathering of your project team helps set the tone of teamwork from the very beginning. For a relatively small investment of time, you can achieve a lot in terms of communication and, at the same time, help avoid misunderstandings about the purpose of the project, team member participation, and authority/responsibility levels.

Example

The accounting department manager was assigned the project of establishing departmental budgeting procedures. This included meeting with every department manager and identifying budget problems in the past, then developing procedures to document budget assumptions for the future. However, none of the department managers were informed that the project even existed. When the project team members showed up to interview department managers, it caused confusion, suspicion, and resentment. The project was off to a poor start.

This project would have been easier to execute if the project manager had held an initial meeting that included department managers. This meeting would have been an opportunity to explain the assignment, the procedures that would be followed, and the probable end result.

If you receive a project assignment, begin with an announcement meeting that includes all members of the team and all departments affected. Also, ask your supervisor to attend and explain the project to the attendees. Once everyone knows what you are doing and why, as well as where the project originated, your job will be much easier.

If your idea for an announcement meeting meets with resistance, explain why the meeting is important with these three points:

1. Announcing a new project defines it for everyone involved and clarifies the intended purpose. The time invested in the meeting will save a lot more time later on.

2. The meeting helps ensure success because everyone gets the message at the same time and from the same source. Your ability to lead the team is aided greatly when the project is launched from the top.

3. A demonstration of executive support for the project manager helps the team achieve its goals. However, it is also necessary to let others in on the decision when they will be affected by the project's outcome.

If you have identified your project team by the time the announcement meeting takes place, it makes it easier to explain the scope of the project to other managers, supervisors, and department members. There is, however, an important difference between trying to complete a project task that conflicts with departmental routines and working with other managers to resolve problems. There are two classifications of managers who will be affected by your project:

■ Those whose procedures will be affected by the outcome of your project

▓ Those supervising employees who will also be a part of your project team

The crossover issues involved with project management can be the most difficult to resolve, so inviting those managers to your announcement meeting is a smart idea. The alternative is to face continual struggles, conflicts, and even resentment from other managers.

Setting Project Objectives

Once your project has been launched, how do you get your team members to work together? Appointing people and handing out assignments is only the beginning. Communication between the project manager and the rest of the team is the only way to ensure that your project is going to succeed.

After the announcement meeting (which should be attended by all affected managers and external resources), you next need an initial core team meeting. Attendees are those people who will be doing the actual work on the project and coordinating the contributions of all outsiders. Obviously, your project will never get off the ground if you hold an endless series of meetings; therefore, this second meeting should be brief and limited, and afterward, there may be little or no actual meetings whatsoever. This meeting has the purpose of identifying how each team member will take part in the overall work. The agenda should be limited to five points, as listed in Figure 3-4 and explained here:

1. *List the problems the team will solve.* Start with a list of your own and invite team members to add to it. Different points of view will help you to better define your objectives in the project.

2. *Offer solutions the team should achieve.* After identifying problems, try to match up likely solutions. This defines the basic work of the project. Ask the team to propose alternatives and expand on your list. This exercise also helps to define the team's approach to the work ahead.

Figure 3-4. Agenda for an initial project meeting.

1. List the problems the team will solve.

2. Offer solutions the team should achieve.

3. Describe information the team will need.

4. Propose initial assignments.

5. Plan the entire project in advance.

3. *Describe information the team will need.* Write down information you need to find out and identify your possible sources. Again, ask the team members to add to your list.

4. *Propose initial assignments.* Identify task areas and suggest which team members you believe are best suited to take responsibility for them. However, don't finalize any assignments at this point. This is supposed to be an initial planning and brainstorming meeting only. Allow team members to define their own roles as much as possible, which will encourage participation.

5. *Plan the entire project in advance.* Establish the initial division of responsibility. This gives the team a good idea of the overall scope of the project. Later, when you put together a schedule and budget, you can fine-tune this step in consultation with team members. You can then take into account any scheduling conflicts and strive for a fair division of workload.

Developing the Initial Schedule

Once you have drafted the preliminary division of responsibilities, you will have a fair idea of how the project will proceed. At this point you can develop your first draft of a schedule. This should be divided into phases. A worksheet for the schedule is provided in Figure 3-5.

Begin with two dates: start (i.e., first meeting) and completion. In between, you will need to identify logical phases (including responsi-

Figure 3-5. Initial schedule.

Date	Description
_____	First meeting
_____	Definitions:
	Purpose: _____
	_____
	Tasks: _____
	_____
	Schedule: _____
	_____
	Budget: _____
	_____
	Phases:
_____	_____
_____	_____
_____	_____
_____	_____
_____	_____
_____	_____
_____	_____
_____	Review
_____	Completion

bility for completion among team members) and a realistic deadline for each phase.

Some phases can overlap. This provides some flexibility in the schedule. When two or more team members are working independently, it is not always necessary for one phase to be completed before some of the work on another phase can begin. What may seem a tight deadline at first glance can be loosened up considerably with some overlapping. At the same time, it is also helpful to allow flexibility; if one phase falls behind, it may be possible to catch up in a subsequent phase.

Your initial schedule should include deadlines for the following items:

- Definition of the project's purpose, tasks, scheduling, and budget

- Identification of each project phase

- Review of completed phases

- Completion (e.g., preparation of a report, documentation, forms, and other project results)

Remember that this is the preliminary schedule for the project, intended only to give you a general idea of the scope of the project. You need to maintain flexibility at this point because as your team begins to develop its own ideas about the scope of the project, the schedule will need to be modified.

After the initial review of the schedule, you need to develop a more comprehensive phase and task listing that includes the final schedule, information sources and types, and a budget. As you move from a preliminary to final schedule, ask team members for suggestions.

Identifying Key Elements Necessary for Project Success

If you begin your project with an announcement meeting and an initial project team meeting, you will already have a fairly good idea of the project's scope. Now you need to identify the elements needed to achieve your goals. These include information resources, a budget, and commitment from your team members.

Information

The first element is information resources. Raw data and other information will come from other departments, existing reports or studies, and outside sources. If the information you need does not exist or is not available to you and your team members, you need to research and develop data on your own.

Analyze your information requirements by answering these questions:

■ ***What sources can supply available information, and what information will have to be developed by the project team?*** If information already exists, identify it and make use of it. Developing your own information bank takes time and resources that can be better spent on other project phases.

■ ***How will we verify information?*** Be aware that someone else's information may be out of date, inaccurate, or contain the wrong emphasis. If your conclusions will be based on information supplied by someone else, you need to be able to check original sources and verify its accuracy.

■ ***How much time will it take to get information from an outside source?*** Build time into your schedule to allow for delays between the request for and delivery of information.

■ ***How much time will it take to study and arrange the information we receive or develop?*** Getting the information is just the first step. Translating raw data into useful information takes a considerable time commitment; this activity has to be built into your project schedule. How will the team approach and interpret information? Establish standards for the objective analysis of information. Strive to remove bias from your work so that your conclusions are objective. Use the scientific method. The scientific method is an approach to research that ensures objectivity and tests results without built-in bias. It can be used in business as well as in the laboratory. The workings of the scientific method require precise and specific working steps to ensure complete objectivity. It begins with definition and clarification; then it involves steps to ensure that the test is valid and appropriate. For example, applied to a market survey, you would want to make sure you sampled typical consumers to see whether a product would be purchased by them. If your sample population does not represent the larger population as a whole, then the sampling data will be wrong as well.

The problem of ensuring that the hypothesis of a test is valid is, perhaps, the most difficult part of any test; the scientific data goes on to document the methods used by the testing group to ensure objectivity and to prove whatever conclusions are reached. By following the rules from beginning to end of the process, you ensure consistency and reliability in the final conclusion. It is further explained on the website http://teacher.nsrl.rochester.edu/phy_labs/AppendixE/AppendixE.html.

Budget

Your project budget should be planned with staffing and information sources in mind. Will you need to buy equipment, pay for outside information, cover travel expenses, or print up a final report? If you need to develop illustrative material, what is the cost? In other words, you need to think of everything. The project budget is just like a departmental budget, except that you have no historical spending pattern for reference.

Maximum control will be possible if you break down your budgeting process by project phase. In that way, you can monitor actual versus budgeted expenses as the project proceeds. Without this feature, you will have difficulty controlling overall expenses. Your objective should be to identify variances as soon as they occur and take steps to correct the problem and prevent further overruns.

In addition, plan for a budget review process. Will you break down each project phase and compare budget to actual? Will you delegate budget review? And what steps will you take if you discover overruns?

Team Commitment

The level of motivation among your core team members defines the entire project. You can lead by example by maintaining a sense of participation and commitment. But also be aware of these factors:

■ *Day-to-day commitments.* Team members have to continue executing their own departmental routines as well as respond to your project requirements.

■ *Priorities.* If team members view projects as impositions on their schedules, it will be difficult to inspire and lead them. Preliminary planning, responsibility assignments, and a participative management style help alleviate this problem.

■ *Coordination.* If you can demonstrate through organizational ability and preplanning that you will help team members work well together, they will be more likely to respond in a positive manner. However, if they sense that the process is poorly defined, that objectives are not spelled out, or that procedures are inefficient, you will not achieve a coordinated team effort.

■ *Leadership support.* As project manager, your emphasis should be on coordinating the team's efforts, staying on schedule, and meeting your budget. Beyond that, you also need to support team members in varying degrees. Some people may work well alone, whereas others will need to be trained and walked through their assignments. Expect team members to look to you to help them solve task-related problems, understand how to approach their assignments, overcome resistance from outside sources, and manage their own scheduling conflicts.

. . . .

Your project will work best when you invest energy and time in planning thoroughly—before the project actually begins. Teams function well when the leader defines and organizes the task ahead and when the end result is explained clearly and agreed upon by the whole team. This is possible only when you choose the best people for the job; the specific team should be an appropriate match for the project. Chapter 3 explores the selection of team members and identification of areas of responsibility.

WORK PROJECT

1. Describe a project team situation where the use of the direct team structure is appropriate, and explain the advantages of this system.

2. Describe the types of project teams that are better managed using the organizational team structure. Compare this method to the direct team structure.

3. List the five topics that should be included on the agenda of the initial project meeting.

4

Choosing the Project Team

You can make more friends in two months by becoming
interested in other people than you can in two years by trying to
get other people interested in you.

—DALE CARNEGIE—

"I don't think I'm going to enjoy myself working on this project," an employee told a friend. "We just finished up our first meeting, and the manager talked the whole time about teamwork."

"Then why are you so worried?" the friend asked.

"It wasn't what he said that disturbed me," the first one replied. "It was those steel marbles he played with the whole time."

The members of the core team ultimately determine whether or not a project succeeds. Whether it's a troop of Boy Scouts or the crew of an aircraft carrier, everyone on the team needs to agree on common goals before they can work together.

The larger your team and the greater its diversity, the more complicated your project management task. A team with only two members—

one leader and one subordinate—involves a singular line of communication. A team consisting of people from several departments involves more complex communication, as well as the opportunity for conflicts in goals and motives.

The Imposed Team Problem

As the theory goes, a project manager is named and allowed to gather a team of his or her own choosing. In practice, however, teams can be selected before you are even consulted.

At the time you receive the project assignment, you may be advised that the team has been selected in advance. For example, an executive may believe the team should be selected at the senior-most level, and the motive may be a worthwhile one. When team members need to be drawn from several different departments, the executive may believe it's easier to gain cooperation from other department managers when the assignment comes from the top. However, an imposed team poses several problems for you as project manager.

If you are given the assignment and team members without the opportunity to be involved in their selection, you start out with a clear disadvantage. If you haven't been allowed to pick individuals for your team, it's also possible that they may not have been given a choice. In addition, it is possible that the people selected may not be qualified, and other department managers may not be happy with the choices, either.

An equally poor situation is created when an executive asks other department managers to pick employees from their departments to serve on your project team. There will be a tendency to select the most dispensable employees for the task, meaning that you will not be provided with the best available team members for the job. Remember, it often happens that a project team consists not of the most capable people, but of the most available. When the project manager does not pick the team participants directly, problems will arise.

To solve the problems associated with the imposed team, consider the list of ideas presented in Figure 4-1 and explained below:

Other Resources

You will find many useful free resources at the Free Management Library. Check the link for "Team Building and Group Leadership" for suggestions on building and managing your team: www.manage menthelp.org/plan_dec/project/project.htm.

1. *Suggest a different approach.* Merely complaining about the methods used to put together the project team is not an effective technique, nor will it lead to improved procedures. It is far more effective for you to offer a solution that makes sense to top management. If you can demonstrate how selecting your own team would improve the quality of the end result, senior management will be more likely to allow you to participate in team member selection.

2. *Do your best with what you are given.* Even when you recommend a more sensible approach, you may still end up with an imposed team. Do your best to define and achieve goals, even if the team is not of the caliber you would have wanted. You can nonetheless make your point to management and ask for a different process in the future; however, once your team has been picked, it is difficult to go back, remove some people, and replace them with others.

Figure 4-1. Guidelines for working with an imposed team.

1. Suggest a different approach.

2. Do your best with what you are given.

3. Give team members the chance to excel.

4. Request team members who work out well.

5. Ask to take part in the selection process.

6. Suggest that department managers should be involved as well.

3. *Give team members the chance to excel.* Just because a team is imposed doesn't always mean that its members are incapable of performing well. Give all team members the chance to do their best work as part of your team. Some people whose performance level is rated low, or who have never been rated, may not have been given the right chance. It is a sad reality that some employees are not given the chance to excel. Everyone deserves the chance to succeed.

4. *Request team members who work out well.* Learn from your own experience. If a team member did well on a past project, request him or her for your current project team. Even if your supervisor does not allow you free rein in naming your team, you may still be able to influence the team selection by stating your preferences.

5. *Ask to take part in the selection process.* You may not have the absolute right to pick your core team, but you should be able to be involved at some level in the selection. Since you are the one who is going to be expected to execute the project, make this point: The team is critical to the success of the project, so you as project manager should have a voice in the selection process.

6. *Suggest that department managers should be involved as well.* Other department managers can be brought in to consult in the selection of your team. The manager of a team member's department should be included in the decision for several reasons. First, these managers have to fill in for lost time when their departmental staff is reduced due to your project; thus, they are in the best position to know how to coordinate the demands of the department versus your project. Second, department managers are in the best position to know who is qualified and experienced in the areas you need on your project. Third, involving managers improves your working relationship with them. No one likes to find out after the fact that their staff has been reassigned, even on a temporary basis. By consulting with them beforehand, even if only as a courtesy, you make your job much easier.

In the most enlightened business environment, upper management provides you with an assignment and then asks you to put together a team. But there will still be restrictions. For example, you probably won't be allowed to recruit core team members from other departments without limitation. It's more likely that you will be free to recruit employees from your own department and request help from others, subject to approval from the top as well as from the affected departments' managers.

The Commitment Problem

Even when a clear schedule is prepared and controlled carefully, when the budget is monitored and overspending is avoided, and when precise project goals are defined, a project can still lack an organized structure.

Some people take the approach that a specific number of bodies are needed to execute the tasks of a project. Under that approach, it doesn't matter who the people are. It only matters that they are able to follow orders and that they have the time to spend on the tasks of the project. This theory is based on the idea that time and labor are commodities, and individual skills are of secondary importance.

The problem, though, is that randomly selected team members, even if they are involved directly with the topic of the project, may not belong on your team for one or more of the following reasons:

- They do not work well with you.

- They do not work well with the rest of your core team.

- They do not have the time available to commit to your project.

- Their department managers do not want to give up the time required.

- The employee is not committed to the project.

- The employee does not have adequate experience to be an asset to the team.

These issues need to be addressed when the suggestion is made to include an individual on your team. Otherwise, the problems will become all too apparent as time progresses. For a team, it takes only one poor fit to derail the whole process.

Your ideal team member will be committed to the project and put in the time and energy to make it succeed. Commitment is not limited to having hours available for the tasks; a valuable team member understands the need for and importance of the end result and is willing to work with you to make the project a success. If that commitment is not there, you will be struggling with the person for the entire time you are working on the project. Chances are you will spend so much time correcting their work, revising it, or assigning uncompleted tasks to other team members that you would be better off with a smaller core team.

You may run into this problem with more than one team member, which makes your problems even more difficult. Unhappy team members not only distract others, but they augment the unhappiness of other members. If people on your team see themselves as anonymous parts of a project for which they will receive no direct credit, they won't be committed to the job. Everyone needs some form of recognition; but because the project is by nature a temporary assignment, many team members will not see how they will benefit from participation. The belief that they will not get recognition prevents them from being committed to the project.

The problem is more than just a negative attitude on the part of core team members. These problems are human and should be expected to some degree. Why should people work hard to make a project succeed if someone else benefits and receives recognition?

As the leader, it's your job to help core team members get beyond the initial attitude that develops in some cases. You need to identify specific features that will give team members a reason to become interested and committed. Real teamwork doesn't happen just by assigning tasks to team members; it is the result of action and opportunity. Action is more than just taking the required steps; it is a forum for the team to develop on its own terms. An absolute requirement is that each team member be given the opportunity to take charge of their part of the project. Once they take ownership, so to speak, people usually also improve their attitude. They will still require supervision, but try to balance oversight with allowing people to apply their initiative and creativity. The question you should ask when putting together your team is, "How can I inspire each person working on this project so that everyone will want to succeed?"

Ten Important Team-Building Guidelines

Every team is different. So even an early success with one team is no guarantee of success with another; too many variables come into the picture. You need to establish a team based on sound leadership and management concepts. These include:

1. ***Determine your own management style and stick with it.*** Team members, like employees in a department, are going to be confused if the manager's style is inconsistent. Find a way to lead that works effectively for you and stick to it. This doesn't mean there are no exceptions, and you may need to remain flexible, especially in a project environment. The landscape may change as you proceed, and in some instances your leadership style will have to evolve as well. But as a general rule, you will need to establish clearly that you are the leader, even when asking the team to participate.

2. ***Make sure your team includes essential members.*** Political motivations often lead to including people who are not needed on the team. Or team members might be added automatically just because you as project manager already supervise them or you have a cordial relationship with them. These are not good reasons for selecting team members. Your team should have all the people it needs, but none of the people it can do without.

3. ***Set goals early and focus work on achieving those goals.*** The project can become chaotic when the circumstances change, and a good leader has to remain focused on the end results that the project needs to achieve. If you set your goals early, communicate them to all team members, and continually use those goals as a basis for your decisions, your project will succeed.

4. *Include the whole team in the plan.* The plan is not a solitary function, and including all of your team in developing the plan allows individuals to take a form of ownership in the project. The outcome is then more important to them, and true team spirit and teamwork are more likely to result. The best teams are those in which the plan of action is developed as a group, not imposed on them.

5. *Use individual talent effectively.* You may select team members based on certain assumptions, only to discover hidden talents once your project is underway. For example, if part of your team is located in Portugal, you might be surprised and happy to learn that one of your local team members is fluent in Portuguese. This can be quite an asset for telephone, e-mail, and other correspondence, and it may help avoid misunderstandings or translation delays. Once you discover talent, use it as efficiently and as effectively as you can.

6. *Recognize individual effort.* A team member or subgroup might excel, developing their tasks quickly, keeping ahead of schedule, or taking the initiative to suggest additional controls or other improvements. When anyone on your team excels in any way, be sure to acknowledge the progress. This means offering praise in front of the entire team, telling the member's supervisor, and documenting the excellent work in reports to management.

7. *Capitalize on what works.* When you find a process that works, whether pertaining to your own leadership style, building teams with members work well together, or approaching problems using brainstorming meetings, stick with it. Teams function best when they find effective ways to work and repeat their success throughout the project.

8. *Always rely on procedures and schedules.* If work gets off track or if unexpected problems and delays arise, decide how to work out the problems by always referring to team procedures and schedules. If you get behind schedule, look for ways to double up on the work to catch up on lost time. Ask team members to make suggestions. Follow procedures whenever possible, but be open to ingenious detours that team members recommend.

9. *Emphasize productivity, even in meetings.* The team will fall apart if it loses momentum. It is boring to take part in a team that falls into a bureaucratic slowdown, and then everyone loses interest. Teams excel when, even as a group, members are allowed to tackle problems, overcome them, and keep moving forward. This is true even in meetings. Some teams work effectively when they are allowed to execute their assigned tasks, but they fall apart if meetings are poorly organized. So all of your team meetings have to be tight, well organized, run from an agenda, and emphasize participation. Try to end meetings early whenever possible, and keep everyone focused on what has to be accomplished—nothing more.

10. *Strive for meetings at the same time and interval.* The meeting is the communications lifeline of every project team. So it has to have a concise agenda, strong leadership, and clear results. Equally important, it helps to make meetings effective when you are able to hold them at the same time every week and for the same duration. For example, you might set the rule that you will meet every Monday from 9:00 to 10:00 A.M. The time should conflict as little as possible with departmental and other duties, but consistency in time and duration helps make the whole project more organized.

Following these guidelines helps team members work together well. Teams do not always operate automatically but are most likely to require firm management and guidance. With this in mind, it pays dividends to determine exactly which individuals or subteam groups are going to be responsible for each phase of your project.

Defining Areas of Responsibility

Successful teams are those that strike a balance between two conflicting attributes: individual initiative versus group needs. On the one hand, each individual wants to believe that he or she has the opportunity to make decisions—the authority to apply talent in coming up with effective solutions. On the other hand, the larger goals of the project must rule, and each individual needs to work with the others as a single team trying to achieve that goal.

How can you achieve a compromise between the desire to satisfy an individual ego and the less personal team priority? The answer is to break out the project tasks into areas of responsibility rather than to merely pass out tasks.

Building a team is very difficult when you are the sole authority for assigning jobs to the bodies in your team. An alternative is to break down the project and refine its phases into distinct assignment ranges, then give each team member the responsibility for executing one or more of those ranges (subject to overall supervision and direction from you).

Example

A project manager in the market research department had experienced difficulty getting team members to work well together. So when a new project was assigned, she took a different approach. Instead of listing project phases and assigning tasks to team members, she identified experienced and dependable team members. She then tried to match responsibilities to each individual. Every phase of the project was scheduled on the basis of responsibility ranges (with listings of tasks within that range). Team members assigned ranges were given considerable freedom to accomplish their roles in terms of working with other team members, meeting deadlines, and solving problems on their own.

There's an important point concerning this approach: As project manager, you need to set boundaries on ranges of tasks while ensuring that each core team member agrees on overall goals. For example, a project team member assigned the role of analyzing and interpreting market test data will need to be told what tests apply and should be directed to meet with you to discuss conclusions before incorporating them into the final report.

The advantage to this approach is that you allow team members to manage their own area of responsibility. Then your role is limited to final approval and to ensuring that the whole team stays on track. You need to stay in touch with team members as they execute their phases, not only to supervise but also to verify that goals are being met. You also fill the needed role of quality control oversight.

The area of responsibility approach grants each individual the full benefit of the doubt in terms of ability to get work done. Some team members will want closer supervision, and you can provide that if necessary. However, this approach is designed to give the greatest degree of incentive possible. It also expresses your confidence in the team. When people believe that they have the greatest amount of freedom, they are more likely to excel in their tasks.

Estimating Time Requirements

Project managers may run into problems because they try to assign tasks rather than broader areas of responsibility. In the belief that a highly structured form of management is preferable in running the project, they overlook the desirability of giving team members a share of the larger job.

Scheduling and assigning are two functions that cannot be separated from one another. They are part of the same process of defining areas of responsibility. The team member who has responsibility for a range of duties can either be told what to do or be given a well-defined end result and then left alone to achieve it.

Although you may give a team member the responsibility for a full phase of the project, it is more likely that you will want to coordinate the phase by defining functions to be executed by the team member. The method you use should depend on timing, the complexity of the phase, and the time requirements for completion, not to mention the team member's ability and desire to execute that part of the job with minimal supervision.

Example 1

One project manager broke down each phase according to the tasks involved. He then met with his team and passed out the schedule, commenting, "This is the list of tasks. You have one week to complete them."

Example 2

Another project manager took a different approach to determining the time requirement for task completion. She first prepared a list of tasks within phases and then estimated the time each would require. She met with the team and asked everyone to provide their own time estimates for task completion.

Whenever conflicts arose, the entire team worked to resolve them. The purpose of this exercise was to identify potential weak links in the schedule and plan for them, with the purpose of doing away with problems that would hold up the entire project. Ultimately, the project manager allowed each team member to determine his or her own time estimate within each phase. The only deadline she imposed was to adhere to the larger project deadline.

Phase flexibility helps team members define their work requirements in the best way, as long as the larger deadline can be met as well. When phases take longer than you would like, you can absorb the difference by overlapping phases where possible. For some projects, entire phases can be broken down by area of responsibility in the same way. For others, one phase will require participation from several team members. In both cases, decisions concerning time demands and deadlines should be set with the team rather than imposed on them. Your role is to ensure that schedule deadlines are met.

Working with Other Departments

One of the potential conflict areas for your project arises whenever you have team members from other departments. You need to ensure that the project's work schedule works well with your team members' departmental deadlines.

Everyone likes to believe that what they are working on today has the highest priority. This causes conflict because other people feel the same way. Remember, though, that a department has one set of deadlines and your project has another. It's not a matter of which priorities are the highest; they are separate. When your schedule comes into conflict with a department's priorities, always assume that the recurring tasks of the department have to come first. There are three reasons for this:

1. *You need the other manager's support.* No matter how the employee ended up on your project team—voluntarily, by imposition, or by agreement with the department manager—remember that your success requires the cooperation of others. In that regard, the department manager is part of your project team, even if participation is limited to support.

2. *A department's work is permanent and your project is temporary.* Keep your project in perspective. Employees from other departments have to continue functioning in their primary role, and they are aware that their manager does their work evaluation, therefore their departmental duties are priorities to them.

3. *Departmental tasks recur and often are tied to specific deadlines.* You have to deal with intermediate phase deadlines as part of an overall project deadline, both of which might be critical. But in addition to the pressure to complete work on their areas of responsibility, team members also have to deal with recurring routines and deadlines in their departments. When setting your schedule, be aware of potential schedule conflicts. Try to anticipate workload problems for team members, such as the close of a monthly cycle, and arrange your deadlines with those team members and their departments in mind.

When conflicts of any nature arise, your first step should be to meet with each department manager and try to work out solutions that satisfy everyone. Avoid placing team members in the middle of a conflict between two demands, project and departmental.

The purpose of meeting with department managers is to resolve conflicts so that they will not recur. Make your position clear: You are meeting because you respect the priorities of the department. You will enlist much greater cooperation by communicating your desire to work with the manager instead of against the goals of that department.

Example 1

The project manager was under pressure to complete the last phase of the project. He was behind schedule, and his boss was demanding the final report. But two of his team members could not complete essential final steps because of deadlines within their departments. The project manager met with the department manager and tried to explain his deadline problems, insisting that the team members be allowed to work on the project first. The department manager would not cooperate.

Example 2

A project manager realized it would be difficult to complete her project on time because of a conflict with another department's deadline. She met with the manager and explained the problem. Together, they came up with a solution that involved recruiting additional help from a third department to relieve deadline pressure for two project team members.

The Executive Point of View

You need to keep in mind the point of view from above. Executives assigning projects may be supportive when you run into problems meeting deadlines, or they may be surprised to hear that you are not able to solve your project scheduling problems.

Given the nonrecurring and uncertain nature of projects, and the cultural environment in many companies, inflexible attitudes about meeting deadlines can be unrealistic. Nonetheless, you may still need to contend with those attitudes. An executive naturally would prefer to give out assignments and walk away, confident that the final report will be delivered on or before the deadline. You may need to solve schedule conflicts on your own, without help from above.

When you realize you cannot make your deadline, it is always best to let your superior know immediately. But don't be surprised if you get one of these responses:

▪ *"It's your project, and you'll have to solve your own prob-lems."* These exact words may not be used, but the message is clear. You were trusted with the assignment, and meeting deadlines is one of the problems you are expected to overcome. Realistically, you would expect credit for delivering the project on time without supervision; by the same argument, the blame would be yours as well if you were late. Adopt the attitude that you are responsible for meeting the deadline, especially if you believe the deadline is realistic. The problems you en-counter along the way are related to your work as a project manager. You will show your ability to work as a project manager by solving the tough problems without extra help. On the other hand, if you believe from the beginning that the deadline is unrealistic, it's your duty to document your belief at the beginning of the project.

▪ *"If you don't get cooperation from another department, let me know and I'll talk to the manager."* While this seems like the most supportive position, be careful. A well-intentioned executive could do more harm than good by bearing down on a manager who is resisting working with you—burning a bridge you might otherwise be able to build with that manager directly. Try to resolve conflicts directly without resorting to help from above.

▪ *"I'd like to help, but there's really nothing I can do."* This message could mean the executive does not want to get in the middle of a conflict. Or it could mean the executive realizes that interceding would cause even more problems, and it's better to require you to solve the problem on your own.

▪ *"Don't make waves. Just do your best to work around the problem."* As passive as this sounds, it could be the best advice of all. Project managers should be results-oriented leaders. At the same time, because their projects affect several departments, they also have to be astute diplomats within the company, getting help while not offending anyone else. If you force another manager to provide employees for your project team, you set your priorities above those of the depart-ment. The consequences of this attitude can be far-reaching and cost you a lot of support, not just for the current project but for future projects as well.

Delegation Problems and Solutions

As a manager, you are familiar with the delegation and monitoring process. As project manager, you need to employ the same skills, but the problems you face may be far different than those you face in a departmental setting. Some common problems and solutions are listed in Figure 4-2. Let's discuss each in more detail.

Making Appropriate Assignments

Problem: Emphasis is on assignments, not on people. As a department manager, you are accustomed to overcoming a series of recurring problems. Your subordinates are permanent, so their task assignments are fixed and well defined. As a project manager, the envi-

Figure 4-2. Delegation problems and solutions.

Problem	Solution
Emphasis is on assignments, not on people.	Pick the right people, not just the right numbers.
A highly structured working environment is imposed on the team.	Encourage individual responsibility and effort.
The leader is too involved and too assertive.	Lead your team in a different way.
The team is isolated due to lack of delegation.	Coach the team, but allow it the freedom to act.
Team members let their egos rule.	Stress team and project goals over individual success.

American Management Association
www.amanet.org

ronment is temporary. Problems are unique to the project and nonre-curring. Your team members do not have well-defined areas of responsibility unless you define them.

Solution: Pick the right people, not just the right number. You may find yourself thinking about projects in departmental terms, and this is a mistake. For example, if you know it takes seven people to manage your department's workload, that doesn't mean that the proj-ect's workload is best defined by the number of people on your team. That should not be your emphasis. An alternative is to pick the people first and then match them to phases and tasks—not by the number of people, but by area of responsibility. If you need more people than estimated at first, they can be added later.

Deciding How Much Structure to Impose

Problem: A highly structured work environment is imposed on the team. You may have learned from experience that a department works well when every task is clearly defined, even before an individual is given a job. The lines of duties are clear in the department. For proj-ects, however, you should encourage team members to think more in-dependently, perhaps with greater freedom than you would want to allow employees in your department. Imposing an overly structured environment on your team members stifles their freedom to act and impedes both creativity and team spirit.

Solution: Encourage individual responsibility and effort. Team members will respond best when they are given a degree of inde-pendence. Teamwork, ironically, often grows by allowing team mem-bers to solve problems as individuals. They may work together better when the restrictions of a department are removed. Give your team the freedom to tackle their areas of responsibility.

Proving Your Leadership Abilities

Problem: The leader is too involved and too assertive. You may be what is called a hands-on manager, someone who likes to roll up your sleeves and do your share of the work. That approach may be appropriate in your department, but for the project, that approach could impede progress. If you insist on doing the project your way, you could prevent the team from forming its own identity. For projects, you might do better with a less assertive approach.

Solution: Lead your team in a different way. Think of your project team in different terms than your department. Reduce your role to that of monitor. Watch the budget and schedule, and supervise only to the degree required by the team. You may need to execute tasks to keep matters on schedule, but as long as your team is able to move matters along without you, let them excel on their own.

Delegating Work Effectively

Problem: The team is isolated through lack of delegation. Project management provides an excellent opportunity for improving your delegation skills. If you do not delegate properly, your team will feel left out of the work of the project. Just as department managers need to keep staff in the loop, you also need to keep core team members involved in operating each phase of the project.

Solution: Coach the team, but allow it the freedom to act. It would be a disaster for a sports team's coach to take the place of a player because the job was not being done properly. If you see one or more team members failing in their area of responsibility, don't step in and take over; work closely with them, not just to help complete the tasks, but also to recognize the phase and project goals. Help your team to succeed instead of allowing delegation to work in reverse.

Identifying Goals

Problem: Team members let their egos rule. You face a difficult challenge when your team stops operating as a unit and becomes a group of individuals in conflict. When team members compete with one another for credit, for work, or for deciding how to proceed, recognize that the problem is not theirs. It is yours. A team running on ego does not function well, but the problem is with the team's leadership. When intended project goals are replaced with individual and personal goals, that means that stronger leadership is needed.

Solution: Stress team and project goals over individual suc-

cess. As the team leader, you are responsible for developing the motives of your team members. You may need to remind individuals more than once that they are working toward a common goal, and that individual credit and recognition have no place on your project team. You can get the point across by example. Don't discuss "your" project; describe it as "our" project, a joint effort. And whenever talking to others about the project, include the team as a whole, and never claim individual credit for the project's success.

. . . .

The personal elements of your project have to be resolved before the budget and schedule can be established and made to work. The structure of your team defines budget and schedule requirements significantly. And your success as project manager rests with the selection of your core team more than with other considerations.

WORK PROJECT

1. List three or more ideas for solving the problem of having a project team imposed on you, and explain how this problem can be solved.

2. Explain why the "area of responsibility" approach is different from assigning tasks to team members.

3. Explain why you should always assume that an outside department's priorities must come first.

Preparing the Project Budget

In every operation there is an above the line and a below the line. Above the line is what you do by the book. Below the line is how you do the job.

—JOHN LE CARRÉ, *A PERFECT SPY*—

"I don't get it," one manager complained to another. "No matter how carefully I budget, my projects always run over. Even when I add a little extra, it gets used up."

The other manager responded, "Maybe you should get out of the business world and go into politics."

If budgeting at any level mystifies and frustrates you, you're in good company. But remember, a budget is only an estimate, and you impose too high a standard on yourself if you expect actual results to match your estimates. The budget is only one of many management tools that you can use to set a standard for measuring results.

Since you do not have a crystal ball for predicting the future, you can only calculate the best possible estimate of expenses based on a reasonable schedule, the resources available to you, and management's expectations. These elements, when properly coordinated, support the development of a realistic budget to guide you through the project maze.

Budgeting Responsibility

The budgeting process creates pressure not only for project managers, but also for departments, divisions, and subsidiaries. There is an implied test of fiscal success built into the budgeting process: If you meet or come in under the budget, you are assumed to be doing a "good job," and if you exceed the budget, you're not.

This is both unfair and unrealistic, even though the assumption is widespread. First of all, a poorly developed budget contains one of two flaws:

1. If expenses are unrealistically low, then failing to meet the budget is not a failure, but a conflict between reality and a poorly drafted budget.

2. If the budget contains generous allowances above a realistic level, then coming in under the budget reveals nothing whatsoever, except that the budget was set at too high a level.

The real purpose of a budget is to set a standard for spending based on the best information you have today—not to meet or come in under that level, but in order to have a means for judging results. When variances occur, it could mean that the budget was in error, or it could mean that expense levels need to be reviewed and brought under control. If you are given a budget that is not unrealistic, it is unfair to hold you to the standard. This problem arises when budgets are imposed on project managers without going through a realistic analysis of expenses that should be expected to occur.

It makes absolutely no sense to use a budget that's been developed without studying the scope of a project. As project manager, you need to develop your own budget for three reasons:

1. *You are responsible for explaining future project expenses and cost variances.* This is possible only when the budget is sensible and based on realistic assumptions.

> **Other Resources**
>
> A series of free articles about project management budgeting can be read or downloaded from the website of Resource Management Systems, Inc. (www.rms.net/project_budgeting_r_pbd.htm).

2. *As project manager, you are in the best position to know what the project should cost.* Your budget is a financially stated goal, and it serves two purposes. First, it provides a means for measuring expenses throughout the project; second, it helps you to measure your own performance as project manager.

3. *You must be able to develop assumptions that support the budgeted numbers.* For your variance analysis and explanation to make any sense, assumptions have to be sensible as well. This is the only way to budget effectively.

Project budgets are developed, monitored, and acted upon differently from budgets for individual departments, subsidiaries, or the whole company. This is so because:

■ ***Projects are nonrecurring.*** Department budgets are prepared annually and often revised every six months (or more frequently). Project budgets are finite, and the budgets are not tied to the fiscal year. (One exception is for the long-term project; when the project term exceeds a full year, its budget could be incorporated into a department's annual budget.) For most projects with a duration under one year, revisions make no sense unless significant errors are discovered in the original budget, or when changes are made to the scope of the project.

■ ***You have more direct control.*** Department budgets often are coordinated between several departments. Fixed expenses may also be allocated among several departments or divisions. However, decisions concerning systems and personnel often are out of the hands of department managers. Projects, however, involve budgeting on two levels.

First is the use of existing resources—personnel and assets—that have been budgeted already at the department level; second is the limited use of outside resources that will not be permanent. When you add a new employee to your department, that's a permanent increased expense to your budget; an additional employee added to your project team is temporary, and usually you'll call upon an employee already on the payroll.

■ *The success of the budget is tied to scheduling and resource performance.* The success of your project budget depends on how well you set and enforce your schedule and each of its phases, and on how well your core team adheres to your schedule. If a phase is delayed, your budget will reflect an unfavorable variance (assuming that payroll expense is separated out from the department's budget and that the project's resource use is measured within your budget).

■ *The cost and profit factors for projects may be more apparent than the same expenses on the departmental level.* Unfavorable variances in your project budget may be subject to more scrutiny than similar or even more apparent unfavorable variances within the department. Because the department budget is considered part of a larger companywide budget and forecast, variances might be overlooked, absorbed by offsetting numbers in other departments, or accepted as inevitable—especially if a department's budget is prepared by a different department, meaning the manager has no control over that budget. But as a project manager, you may be held accountable to a greater degree because you are responsible for achieving the goals of the project. That means not only getting the desired result by the deadline, but keeping to the budget as well.

It's true that the same standards should apply to each department manager. Ideally, the manager should develop the department's budget and then be held accountable for variances. In practice, however, a company may not exercise the level of follow-up that would make budgeting effective. Few companies allow department managers to participate in their budget's development to the degree that accountability would even be possible. The more common practices include having the accounting department prepare department budgets, or having managers prepare preliminary budgets, with executive-level changes to follow. Both of these practices, while common, make no sense.

For project managers, the opportunity to have more control makes budgeting far more interesting. However, that also means that you will be expected to explain why your actual expenses exceed the budget. As a project manager you may be required to handle variance reporting in a much different way than you would as a department manager.

Checklist: Effective Budgets

In preparing your project budget, remember its purpose: to provide limitations and goals that can be monitored. Bringing a project in at or below budget is just as important as it is for expenditures in a department or a division. The budget is too often a mechanical exercise that is not taken seriously or employed properly. It is intended as a measuring device; no project is going to be approved with an unlimited budget, and a properly prepared budget should provide you a means for control.

Keep these principles in mind to create an effective project budget:

1. *The budget has to be realistic.* There is no point in taking the time to prepare a budget unless it realistically describes what your project is going to cost. Some organizations assign a project and a budget without knowing what is involved; this is a mistake. As project manager, your budgetary responsibilities are part of your responsibility. This means that a budget that does not reflect reality is useless.

2. *The more detailed the budget is, the better the project will be.* Break down the costs and expenses of the budget in great detail. Pay close attention to the most important budget item: labor. Too often, project budgets are reflected in a single lump sum, and as a result of having no line items, the control element is lost. You need to know how the budget is going to be spent in order to monitor your own progress.

3. *The budget term should be tied to the project completion month, not to the business cycle.* A common error is to prepare a budget in conformity with a departmental or segment budget. So it ends at the finish of the fiscal year or the next quarter. But every project has its own completion cycle that does not conform to the fiscal cycle.

So be sure your budget reflects the timing of the project schedule, not the better known quarterly or annual organizational budget.

4. *Cost and expense items should be itemized by budget phase.* Just as a departmental budget is itemized by month, your project budget needs to be broken out by completion phase. So you need to know not only how the budget is to be spent, but also when. This is an effective method for judging the schedule itself. Staying on schedule normally keeps labor costs down, whereas time overruns invariably increase labor costs. Naturally, this creates negative budget variances in labor. So in this regard, the phase-specific budget can work not only as a financial management tool, but also as a means for enforcing the schedule.

5. *All underlying budget assumptions should be written down and explained.* Many budgets fail because no one really knows how the numbers are developed. If you expect to be able to understand the causes of any budget variances, you need to write out the assumptions. For example, in the labor category, you need to document the hours and costs for each team member in each phase. If a phase runs over these estimates, you will know where the budget fell short or where costs ran over budget.

6. *When uncertain, include a reserve in the budget.* Many project phases are going to involve cost elements you cannot identify in advance. These tend to emerge as the project progresses, so how do you budget for them? It is never effective to include an expense buffer merely to provide for uncontrolled overruns, but when a phase of the project cannot be fully understood in advance, it is appropriate to create a reserve. This will allow you to create a basic assumption about future phase costs, even if these will have to be revised later as more facts are revealed.

7. *Prepare a variance report, identify the causes of budget problems, and fix them.* Some budgets include the periodic routine of comparing budgeted items to actual and detailing the variances. But these are of only limited value unless two additional steps are taken. First, the variance needs to be analyzed in the context of the original budget's assumptions. Second, discovered flaws in budgetary controls have to be fixed or, if the flaw is in the original assumptions, the budget has to be revised. This analysis should be performed at least once per month, and certainly at the conclusion of each project phase.

8. *If your budget turns out not to be realistic, do a revision.* Many budget revisions are undertaken primarily because cost overruns are excessive. This is not a good reason for a revision, especially if management steps could reduce those costs and bring them into line. However, if and when you find that your project budget is not realistic, a revision should be prepared for the remaining phases. Remember the reasons to prepare a budget: to control costs and expenses, to focus on controllable variances and fix them, and to provide yourself with a financial measurement of the project.

Labor Expense: The Primary Factor

In any discussion of a project budget, top management's first question is, "What will the project cost, and is that reasonable?" If the project is optional, the decision to proceed will probably be based on cost rather than the desirability of having the end result.

The only way to know the cost of the project in advance is to identify the actual expenses. Remembering that your budget is no more than an estimate (an educated guess, in other words), be sure to include labor expenses—the cost of paying members of your team. Although labor is often the largest portion of the project's cost, it often is left out entirely. The thinking is that because existing staff members are used on the project, the payroll expenses occur anyhow—why calculate them for the project? The answer, of course, is that the hours worked on your project are hours taken away from other duties. Labor is a very real expense, even if it remains hidden in a department budget. To calculate the feasibility of doing the project, labor should be counted.

Example 1

A project manager is asked to estimate the expense of hiring an outside consultant, researching historical financial results, and leasing equipment needed for the project. In addition, she is authorized to recruit a team of five employees from other departments. However, payroll for those core team members is not included in the budget.

The real cost of this project depends largely on the time required to complete tasks, and most of that work is going to be performed by employees. In this situation, management does not gain a true picture of the project cost because the most significant cost element is excluded.

Here are three recommendations for project budgeting where labor is concerned:

1. *Don't overlook the labor expense portion of your project.* Even when team members come from within the company, and even though payroll is already budgeted in a departmental budget, the only way to know what a project costs is to include labor. This is true even if labor expenses are developed on a footnote basis; it is important to calculate and report the real project cost.

2. *Don't add a "fudge factor" to labor—or to any other segment of your budget.* Remember, the purpose of your budget isn't to end up within the budget, but to estimate as accurately as possible what it is going to cost. Fudge factors are meant to protect against unfavorable variances, should they occur. But such approaches are contrary to the intended purpose of budgeting.

3. *Develop your labor estimate before selecting your project team.* Labor demands for each project phase dictate the needed size, scope, and capabilities of your team. Estimate total hours required for completion of each phase, broken down by individual. Use a worksheet, such as the one shown in Figure 5-1, to document the hours you require. This defines your resource pool, or your core team needs. You may also need to adjust this estimate after meeting with team members.

Example 2

The manager of a technical support department has several recurring tasks to execute: developing and modifying internal systems, writing documentation, and training employees. The manager was recently given a project assignment to develop user procedures for a newly installed database system used by several processing departments. The manager needs to create a budget and schedule, and has broken the project out into seven distinct phases. Team members are identified as follows:

Figure 5-1. Preliminary labor estimate worksheet.

Project: _____

TEAM MEMBER	PHASE						
TOTAL							

- One employee from the processing department

- One employee from the systems development department

- Three employees from the technical support department, with responsibilities broken down into areas of responsibility for research, documentation, and testing

The manager develops a preliminary estimate of hours required for each of the seven phases. The preliminary estimate looks like this:

Preliminary Labor Estimate (Hours)
Project: Automation, Processing Unit

Team Member	Phase						
	1	2	3	4	5	6	7
Project manager	23	22	8	25	30	24	40
Processing unit	6	18	25	10	5	0	0
Systems development	20	25	25	20	10	5	5
Research	15	15	20	5	0	0	5
Documentation	0	0	10	10	15	20	35
Testing	0	0	0	5	25	15	10
Total	64	80	88	75	85	64	95

Both the estimate of hours and the schedule itself are subject to revision once the team members have reviewed and added their suggestions.

Additional Budgeting Segments

Many projects are characterized exclusively by the labor factor, especially when all tasks are administrative. Management makes a mistake by expecting project costs to be absorbed within a departmental budget without at least studying the cost, both to determine whether it makes sense to proceed and to estimate whether the project is proceeding within budget.

Additional budgeting is required whenever resources and facilities beyond labor will also be involved. Additional budgeting may be required for:

■ *Fixed overhead allocation.* Some companies decide to allocate overhead expenses to departments and may also assign expenses to projects. This is most likely to occur on long-term projects that exceed a single fiscal year, when the project operates much like a department.

Fixed overhead allocations are random by nature and done by formula. For example, departments may be allocated a portion of utilities and maintenance on the basis of square footage in their department or the number of employees. Allocations don't make any sense for projects if, in fact, the project manager's department has already been allocated a portion of fixed overhead. However, if your company's accounting department uses a full cost accounting approach, you may end up having to budget for allocated expenses.

■ *Variable expenses.* Some projects are subject to the same accounting formats used in departments. This means that project-related expenses are broken out and reported apart from the usual department expenses. A long-term project or series of related projects may even be assigned its own cost center in the company books; this is not at all unusual. In this instance, you must budget for variable expenses, both by phase and for the entire project. When a separate cost center is established, your project will be expected to conform to the reporting norms of other cost centers, specifically departments.

■ *Special expenses.* A third area you may need to include in your budget is for special expenses. These costs depend on the nature of your project. For example, you may need to hire an outside consultant, use an independent research company, or lease equipment. Some internal departments will contribute to your project in ways other than providing direct labor. Systems development may supply automated services for testing and running data, for example. If departments break down their nonlabor services by cost, you may need to include those costs in your budget.

It is also possible that a project will require a capital expenditures budget. For example, if your project involves comparing costs and benefits of assets and then purchasing the best ones for use in your company, you'll need to estimate the cost of acquiring assets. In this case, the end result (i.e., asset acquisition) may itself be a budget item.

When a series of projects begins to take on similar attributes, the projects can be executed by formula. They then become more routine than exceptional, and your project management duties begin to look more and more like a departmental operation. Even so, unless your project work actually evolves into its own department, your projects are most likely to be budgeted individually.

Because the majority of projects are unique, you will probably find the budgeting process frustrating. Not only do you need to account for fixed and variable expenses, you'll also discover that some of those allocations are not actually controlled or spent by you. They are merely entries made to account for costs when the real spending occurs in a department. The purpose, once again, is to show what the project costs, not what you have spent. As important as it is to conclusively show the total cost of a project, when you are provided no real control over spending levels, budgeting becomes an exercise in analysis. However, this is a necessary part of the project management routine. Unless your project is of such scope that management is willing to set up a temporary cost center and provide you with your own staff and budget, the project budget will never be as easy to calculate as the budget of a department.

Budgeting Each Phase of Your Project

An effective project budget enables you to monitor progress at each phase and identify exactly when and why actual expense levels vary from your estimate. Thus, your budget is best constructed and defined phase by phase.

All of your budget elements—labor, fixed expenses, and variable expenses—vary according to the requirements of each phase. Some phases will move along quickly and require minimal team involvement and little or no expense. Others will demand many staff hours, involve the use of external resources and facilities, and require more careful monitoring.

To identify problems expressed as budget variances, you need to match actual results to the assumptions underlying your budget. If you assume that a particular phase will require fifteen hours from an outside consultant, but it actually comes in at twenty-two hours, you will be able to identify the exact cause of the variance.

Breaking down your budget by phases also allows you to identify timing problems, time overruns, and miscalculations of the scope of a particular phase. The breakdown is mandatory for budget monitoring. Some expenses may come in under budget while others run over. Some expenses will occur earlier or later than expected. Identifying the causes of variances requires matching original estimates of phase completion costs with actual outcomes.

If your project is set up with labor as the major expense factor, then actual hours spent should also be matched to the percentage-of-completion of the whole project. In other words, if 30 percent of total labor hours are budgeted for the first four phases, a variation from that match could spell a budget problem in future phases as well. Labor hours and costs can serve as the central point for budget monitoring.

Example

In the preliminary labor estimate of your project, seven phases were identified, with estimates for total labor hours per phase. To identify the budgeted percentage-of-completion level for each phase, divide the number of hours in each phase by the total estimate of labor hours and round to the nearest full percentage, as follows:

Phase	Hours	Percentage (%)
1	64	12
2	80	14
3	88	16
4	75	14
5	85	15
6	64	12
7	95	17
Total	551	100

Assuming that nonlabor expenses will follow labor trends, the rest of the project budget can be designed along labor-hour lines. When expenses occur at levels different from the labor trend, a variance report should be footnoted to explain the discrepancy. However, if you know in advance that a particular expense won't follow the labor trend, that information can be separated out. For example, if you plan to hire a consultant for the first phase of the project, it makes sense to include the budget for that expense in the first phase rather than spread out among all phases.

A percentage-of-completion variance report is prepared on the basis of project phases completed to date. A worksheet for this type of variance report is shown in Figure 5-2.

The estimated percentage-of-completion for each phase is cumulative. Thus, in our example, at the end of phase two, completion should be at 26 percent (12 plus 14); and at the end of phase three, it should rise to 42 percent (12 plus 14 plus 16).

Taking this a step further, let's assume that the project's budget is broken down into these groups:

Labor	$8,200
Variable expenses	1,250
Consulting	2,000
Total budget	$11,450

Figure 5-2. Variance report worksheet.

Variance Report

Date: _____

Project: _____

Completion: _____ %

Description	Budget	Actual	Variance	
			Amount	**%**
	$	$	$	%
Total	$	$	$	%

A completed worksheet at the end of the third phase (i.e., 42 percent completion) may look as follows (amounts have been rounded to the nearest $25):

Variance Report

Date: 5/31 _____

Project: Automate processing unit _____

Completion: 42% _____

Description	Budget	Actual	Variance	
			Amount	**%**
Labor	$3,450	$3,135	$ 315	10.0
Variable expenses	525	615	(90)	(14.6)
Consulting	840	0	840	100.0
Total	$4,815	$3,750	$1,065	28.4

The Budget column is computed by multiplying the total budget by the indicated percent completed (i.e., 42 percent). Actual expenses to date are compared to project-to-date budget. A favorable variance (i.e., when actual is lower than budget) appears without parentheses; an unfavorable variance (i.e., when actual exceeds budget) is shown in parentheses. (In this example, the consulting expense is assumed to be budgeted in early phases, but payment for those services has not yet been made). Variance percentage is the variance amount divided by the actual column.

Accompanying this variance report is a full explanation of variances in each category. For example, the labor budget explanation may be broken down by team member and with an analysis of phase completion levels versus original assumptions.

Remember that the purpose of this exercise is to identify potential problems. The overall variance can be meaningless unless its components can be isolated and identified. As project manager, you may not need to formalize the process of variance analysis unless your project involves a large budget and many team members. The report examples provided in this chapter are intended to demonstrate how the analysis occurs, not the precise format required in every case.

To study labor variances by team member or, more precisely, by function performed, break down actual versus budget and perform the same comparison you used for the total budget. An example follows:

Labor Variance (Hours)

Team Member	Hours, Project-to-Date		
	Budgeted	Actual	Variance
Project manager	53	37	16
Processing unit	49	42	7
Systems development	70	61	9
Research	50	71	(21)
Documentation	10	8	2
Testing	0	0	0
Total hours	232	219	13

The initial three phases required less time than anticipated for organizing and defining automation requirements. This was offset by higher than expected research time demands.

The example used here shows how and why labor variances occurred; it also shows that variances can be absorbed during future phases, or that miscalculations in original estimates cause variances in many instances. The problem may not be limited to completed phases but may continue through additional phases as well. You may also discover that a final deadline will not be met because of overruns in the hours required for particular functions (such as research in the aforementioned example).

The hours variance is fairly easy to analyze; the study can also be translated into dollar amounts if necessary. If you are required to report your project's budget variances as part of a periodic review, it will be necessary to report the dollar amounts of variances in labor.

Budgeting Controls

Variance reporting may occur in two ways: You can present a report summarizing the status of your project, with explanations of variances (provided to management as part of the oversight function), or you can use the procedure yourself to track the budget and take corrective action where possible. The latter is an important part of your project management routine even if you are not required to make interim reports during the execution of the project.

Here are some examples of budgeting problems you may encounter, with corrective actions you can take.

Labor Expenses Exceed Budget

The cause of this problem may be that phases are taking longer than you anticipated. Several actions may be appropriate:

Solution 1: Examine the budgets for remaining phases to determine if they are realistic. If not, revise the entire budget to reflect a realistic likely outcome.

Solution 2: Determine whether any unfavorable variances can be absorbed in future phases. In some cases, project-to-date variances are the result of advance work for future phases. In this instance, the variance is nothing more than a timing problem.

Solution 3: Check your level of supervisory involvement. It may be necessary to work more closely with core team members to ensure that they are working efficiently.

Variable Expenses Exceed Budget Levels

This problem may occur because original assumptions were wrong, or because you are not exercising appropriate control over spending. Consider these actions:

Solution 1: Check original assumptions against experience to date. Are the assumptions still valid? If not, revise the budget.

Solution 2: Determine whether any of the expenses to date will be absorbed during later phases. If so, the variance is due to timing differences.

Solution 3: Initiate needed controls just like you enforce spending limits in your department. For a long-term project, controls could involve preapproval of requisitions or check requests.

Expenses Are Lower Than Budget, and Not Due to Timing

Some project managers budget conservatively in their departments yet build in safety levels in their project budgets. This, too, can be problematic and requires corrective action:

Solution: If you have added a "fudge factor" in your budget, revise it and remove the excess. The fudge factor defeats the purpose of project budgeting. Your budget isn't meant to anticipate actual spending levels, but only to establish an assumed reasonable level for the purpose of future comparisons. Thus, a safety factor prevents you from exercising any meaningful controls.

* * * * * * * * * * *

Remember, it is the nature of budgets to become increasingly inaccurate as time passes. They are nothing more than your best estimate. You should never expect actual expenses to match your budget. However, that budget can be used as a standard for judging how well you are able to control expense levels throughout your project. Your purpose in estimating expenses is not to know ahead of time how much you are allowed to spend, but to create that standard.

WORK PROJECT

1. You are preparing a labor budget for your project. You have defined four separate phases, and your team contains five members. The following table summarizes your initial estimate of hours. What is the percentage-of-completion for each phase? Show individual phases and cumulative percentages.

| | Phase | | | |
Team Member	1	2	3	4
1	10	15	15	25
2	8	8	6	12
3	0	15	25	20
4	0	20	20	25
5	10	5	10	15
Total	28	63	76	97

2. Your team members earn varying amounts on a per-hour basis. Those amounts are broken down and presented in the table that follows. Calculate the total dollar amount of labor budget for each phase of the project.

Team Member	Hourly Payroll
1	$20.00
2	15.00
3	18.00
4	9.00
5	10.00

3. You have estimated a total of $2,800 for nonlabor expenses during your project. Based on labor percentage-of-completion (hours), what is the nonlabor budget for each phase?

Establishing a Schedule

*We are continually faced with a series of great opportunities
brilliantly disguised as insoluble problems.*

—JOHN W. GARDNER—

The project manager called a team meeting for 9:00 A.M. the next morning. "Don't be late," he said sternly. "We'll be discussing the project schedule."

The team assembled promptly at 9:00 as instructed. But the manager was nowhere to be seen. At 9:20, one of the team members called the manager's home and asked for him.

"He'll be a little late this morning," the manager's wife explained. "He missed the bus."

Your project ran over budget, you didn't have the right people on your team, and you missed the final deadline. In fact, you went on vacation so you wouldn't be there when your boss found out.

If this describes your experience with projects in the past or your fear about future ones, then you need to find effective ways to plan and control your schedule. In a sense, the schedule is a budget for time. If you do not plan, coordinate, and control the schedule, you probably will not make the final deadline, either. Scheduling techniques, when applied in the project environment, can help anticipate and solve problems, get the team working together, and advance each project with the final deadline in mind.

In creating a schedule, you will need to apply five skills:

1. *Task definition and team function.* Every task is related to a series of other tasks in a project's phase, and each phase is related to all other phases. In addition, every team member's efforts affect every other member's. This means that exceptional work helps, but slow, incomplete, or error-prone work hurts everyone else. To succeed with your schedule, you will need to define carefully each task and how each team member functions as part of the overall team.

2. *Risk management.* Remember that risk exists everywhere and by definition is invariably a surprise. The degree to which you are able to anticipate risk and then prevent it or mitigate its effects will ultimately determine how well your project succeeds. As project manager, you need to be continually aware of this and to look for potential threats to the smooth operation of your schedule.

3. *Organization of tasks in detail.* In the next chapter, the concept of Work Breakdown Structure (WBS) is examined in detail. The greater the effort you put into defining tasks as an outline of the project, the greater your chances will be of (a) creating a realistic schedule, (b) completing each phase on time, and (c) responding to delays to get effectively back on schedule.

4. *Realistic time estimates.* Just as expense budgeting is uncertain, your estimate of the time required to complete each task and each phase is going to determine whether you can complete your project on time. In other words, the more time you invest in creating scheduling assumptions, the more likely it will be that your schedule will work out.

5. *Effective use of resources.* Some projects can be operated with a small, local team. This is fairly easy compared to a broader proj-

ect involving many outside resources or remote team members. In either case, project management and scheduling rely heavily on your ability to effectively identify, call upon, and apply all of the resources you need. This usually means personnel in the form of team members but may also include outside expertise and even nonpersonnel resources (equipment or information technology data, for example).

The Scheduling Problem

If you could work as a team of one, you wouldn't need to coordinate other people's efforts and phase deadlines. Instead, you could plan, control, and achieve the end results of the project all on your own.

When working with a team, however, your schedule is the "crunch point" for the whole team. Their networking requirements work on at least three levels: with one another, with you as the project manager, and with their recurring departmental tasks. Even at the beginning of your project, the schedule can get off track. For example, the entire core team may agree on your schedule and proceed with phase one, but it would take only one unexpected delay to throw off the entire schedule. Without your continual supervision, such delays certainly arise. Even when you supervise carefully, you need to be prepared for the unexpected.

A small delay within one phase would not be a problem if the shortfall could be absorbed within subsequent phases. But chances are that a single delay near the beginning of the project will carry over in further delays affecting all phases yet to come. Keep these five important points in mind concerning delays:

1. *Every delay affects scheduling for the remainder of the project.* Some projects start out with chronic delays from the very beginning. If you don't begin phase one on the scheduled start date, you have already encountered a problem that is likely to carry through to other phases. Be sure that your schedule is realistic and then follow it faithfully. Your ability to keep the project on schedule is a real test of your project management abilities.

2. *To meet your deadline, the delay has to be absorbed in a later phase.* It's always desirable to build a little flexibility into your schedule by allowing more time than you think you will need for completion. However, when a deadline has been imposed on you, that luxury is not always possible. Chances are you'll have enough problems meeting the deadline without any opportunity for moving delays to future phases. If a delay takes place in an early phase, your team will have to make up the lost time somewhere along the way.

3. *It's always desirable to meet the final deadline, unless that means the outcome will be incomplete, inaccurate, or otherwise short of the desired result.* To make up for a delay, you may need to accelerate the team's work schedule, look for shortcuts in the original plan, or put in more core team hours. So delays usually translate into labor budget overruns. Your goal should be to meet the promised deadline unless that means cutting down on quality and thoroughness of the result. Your project should end up with the highest possible quality report, implemented procedure, or other outcome—even if that requires asking for a deadline extension.

4. *Staying on schedule and meeting the deadline is the project manager's job.* If you miss your deadline, you may be asked for an explanation. Remember that delays are your responsibility, regardless of the cause. Project managers are expected to monitor progress; in fact, that should be high on the list of your functions in that role. You also are expected to anticipate problems before they create delays and take action to offset those problems. Never blame team members or outside forces for delays when explaining missed deadlines; you are the project manager and that responsibility goes with the job.

5. *When schedule delays are beyond your control, the final deadline has to be kept flexible.* Some projects require interim review and approval before you can proceed. For example, your project might proceed to a point where a preliminary report is prepared and submitted for approval. If your supervisor does not get back to you by a deadline, then the final deadline for your project has to be pushed forward. In developing your schedule, keep in mind which deadlines are within your control and which ones are not.

Your initial schedule can be summarized in chart form, which helps you to visualize the progress of each phase. Visualized schedule control is an effective tool for project managers. It also helps your core team to understand and to see how the project is progressing against the schedule. Your chart should report both planned and actual timing of phase completion, and it serves several purposes:

- It works well as your primary tracking tool, especially in the early phases.

- It provides core team members with scheduling guidance, which works as a visual expression of your project goals.

- It gives everyone on your team an ongoing view for spotting and overcoming emerging problems.

The schedule chart also helps you monitor your project methodically—a task that, without some form of planning aid, is formidable. The overall scope of a project can be complex; charting the phases helps isolate and solve problems while keeping the entire schedule moving along. The final deadline can be met only when you also meet a series of smaller deadlines along the way, which also means absorbing small delays as a means of avoiding big ones.

The Gantt Chart

Initial scheduling is effectively planned and tracked by the use of the Gantt chart. This device, also called the timeline chart, was developed and used by industrial engineer and management expert Henry Gantt.

Gantt worked with the Army Bureau of Ordnance during World War I, when he was faced with the task of controlling munitions production. He realized that by breaking down the process into precise phases, control would be easier and several phases could be executed at the same time in whole or in part. Gantt also understood that this idea could be best communicated to others visually. The visual display chart he developed has come to be known as the Gantt chart.

The chart can be constructed using boxes, lines, or symbols. It shows comparative completion status for several phases, comparing planned start/stop dates to actual; it also shows where phases can overlap one another. Phases are listed from top to bottom and completion schedule and actual durations are shown from left to right.

The chart can be developed by hand or on a computer spreadsheet. Numerous scheduling and project management software programs include Gantt chart management as part of their programs. The chart is most effective when it is used both by the project manager and by team members in planning, controlling, and operating the project.

Finding the Best Scheduling Software

Nicely designed scheduling software is often found as part of a broader application. *Software Magazine* (www.softwaremag.com) tracks newly developed programs and offers. Also check the following for software designed specifically for scheduling:

Computer Associates   www.ca.com
Microsoft Project   www.microsoft.com/en-us/project
Open Plan Professional   www.welcom.com

To illustrate the best use of the Gantt chart, let's work through a sample project. The use of black-and-white boxes or bars is the most easily comprehended and used form of the Gantt chart. For this reason, our example is shown using this simplified Gantt system.

Example

The accounting department manager undertakes a project to examine current procedures in the accounts payable department. She will identify changes needed to improve efficiency and reduce processing expenses, concluding with the implementation of revisions. Her team consists of the accounting department assistant manager, the supervisor of accounts payable, and a senior-level employee from the systems development department.

The manager's first step is to break down the project into phases, as follows:

Phase 1   Document current procedures for each of three employees in the department.
              Estimated completion time: four days

Phase 2   Prepare procedure flowcharts for the department.
              Estimated completion time: three days

Phase 3   Summarize paper flow and methods for receiving, processing, and sending out information (including timing, approval, and payments).
              Estimated completion time: five days

Phase 4   List problem areas and develop initial recommendations for solutions.
              Estimated completion time: six days

Phase 5   Develop improved processing procedures.
              Estimated completion time: three days

Phase 6   Track sample transactions for one week under existing procedures.
              Estimated completion time: five days

Phase 7   Track sample transactions for two weeks under proposed new procedures.
              Estimated completion time: ten days

Phase 8   Prepare and deliver a final report to the treasurer, including recommended changes in procedures, estimate of savings, and automation, if applicable.
              Estimated completion time: two days

This listing of phases can be expressed on a Gantt chart using the most common method, the bar chart. The schedule for this project, including both planned and actual completion for each phase, is shown in Figure 6-1.

In Figure 6-1, note that the planned phases are shown as white or

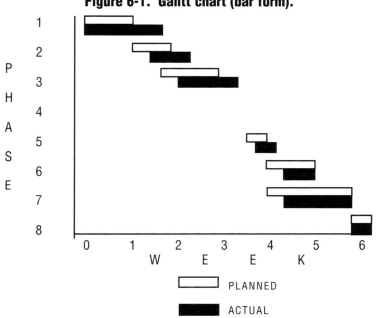

Figure 6-1. Gantt chart (bar form).

clear bars, and actual completion ranges are filled in black. This method shows where delays occurred during execution of the project; it tells both the project manager and team members that these delays need to be absorbed later on. Phase 1, for example, took longer than scheduled, thus delaying phase 2. That delay carried through all the way to phases 6 and 7, where it was absorbed by abbreviating the tracking periods.

Some phases can be run concurrently. For example, the longest phases (6 and 7) involved testing (i.e., tracking) current and proposed procedures. These tests are conducted over the same period, saving a full week. In this example, both test periods were shortened slightly to bring the project back on schedule, in the belief that a shortened test period would not compromise the project.

Scheduling Control

The more planning you put into developing your initial schedule, the better your chances for meeting deadlines, both for phases and the

Guidelines for Selecting Project Scheduling Software

Can software for project scheduling save time and effort? An investment in well-designed scheduling software is worthwhile as long as it saves time for you and your team. In comparing available products, consider these guidelines:

- *Cost*. It is possible to find effective and efficient software without buying the highest-priced products. However, going for the cheapest software usually means you lose some desirable features. Seek out the best possible midrange software, a product that offers all of the features you need to track schedules.

- *Ease of Use*. It is worth paying a little more to get a product you can learn quickly. Compare tutorials, wizards, and interface design. Visit websites for the major software suppliers and try out demo software if available.

- *Charting Resources*. Remember that scheduling is best managed visually. Choose software that includes Gantt charting and enables you to customize fields. Drag-and-drop graphical features save time and improve the quality of your visual presentations.

- *Integration Features*. Does the software enable you to transfer scheduling and other project management features into text documents such as reports? A project management software product that also supports preparation of a final report serves multiple purposes.

final project. Plan to review your proposed schedule with each and every core team member. Make sure that each member agrees that the schedule is reasonable and that deadlines can be met.

Follow these steps (summarized in Figure 6-2) to create your project schedule:

1. *Identify phases*. Break down your project into logical and sequential phases. Definable areas of effort and team responsibility should distinguish each phase. Each phase should also be characterized

Figure 6-2. Creating the schedule.

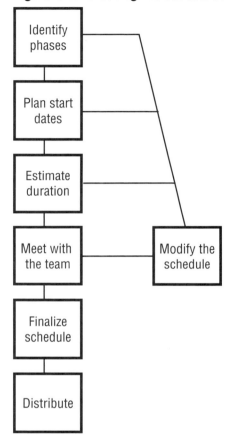

by a result, its dependence on prior phase completion, and its necessity for phases yet to come.

    *2. **Plan start dates.*** Decide which phases must be executed consecutively and which can be executed concurrently. In some cases, a phase cannot begin until a previous phase has been completed. In others, two or more different phases can proceed at the same time.

    *3. **Estimate the duration of each phase.*** Next, decide how many days will be needed to complete each phase. Basing your schedule on a preliminary estimate of labor hours is an acceptable preliminary method; however, before finalizing the schedule, convert hours to days, keeping in mind the probability that team members will have to split time between project and departmental duties.

4. *Meet with the team.* Involve your team members in schedule planning to ensure that they will work together cooperatively and that each member believes the schedule is practical, given the restraints of time and other duties.

5. *Modify the schedule as needed.* Listen to what your team tells you. If members believe that a phase deadline is unrealistic, look for solutions. Modify the schedule according to the team's response.

6. *Prepare the schedule.* Construct a Gantt chart for your final schedule, and plan to use it to track your progress. As the project moves along, actual start and finish dates for each phase are entered on the chart.

7. *Distribute the schedule.* Upon finalizing your schedule and Gantt chart, provide copies of both to each team member. As the project moves ahead, pass out revised and updated copies periodically to remind team members of the schedule and to help them visualize progress. If you are also required to report to upper management on the schedule of the progress, include the Gantt chart in your report.

The Scheduling Solution

Even the most efficient, experienced, and capable project manager will be faced with serious schedule delays. The delay itself is not a failure of the process; it simply is part of the team dynamic. The real test is found in how the manager solves the problem when it does occur.

Problems often can be spotted in advance of a delay, and action taken to prevent it. For example, if a team member tells you before a phase begins that it will be impossible to meet the deadline, the task needs to be shifted to someone else. It often occurs that departmental demands prevent team members from putting in the time they originally thought they would have available for the project. As long as team members keep you updated when such problems occur, you can shift work to other team members and avoid the delay.

Once a delay has occurred, you need to take one of these steps to fix the problem:

■ ***Execute phases concurrently when possible, even if your original schedule called for consecutive completion.*** Some phases, or segments of phases, can be started early. Get your team working together to do as much advance work as possible, saving time later and absorbing a delay.

■ ***Double up the team's efforts to absorb a previous delay.*** If team members have time available today, a schedule can be accelerated to speed up completion time. A day or two saved on subsequent phases can do away with earlier delays.

■ ***Look for ways to speed up future phases.*** It may be possible to shorten time requirements in future phases in several ways. You can recruit additional employee help for especially time-consuming phases; shorten test phases; or abbreviate a research phase without compromising quality. On some projects, parts of a final report can be drafted in advance so that the final phase can be completed in less time than originally planned.

Gantt Limitations

The Gantt chart is a useful visual tool for tracking your project and anticipating delay problems before the final deadline is compromised. However, it will be of limited use when you have to deal with a relatively large project team. In those instances, there is likely to be a high volume of interaction and the need for cooperation between individuals on your core team. The more complex the team structure, the higher the likelihood of schedule delays. And the longer the term of the project, the more problems you are likely to encounter keeping on schedule.

Remember, charting phases and monitoring progress is only a tool, not the solution itself. The chart reveals where problems are occurring. For more complex projects, the Gantt chart has a few limitations:

■ *It does not identify potential weak links between phases.* Whenever the flow of work transfers from one person to another, there is the potential for delay. This is especially true when a phase ends and another is about to begin. These are the weak links in your schedule. You can control your schedule by identifying the transfer points within phases and from one phase to another, then ensuring that the flow of work continues without a break.

■ *The chart does not reveal team problems due to unexpected delays.* The Gantt chart only shows the planned and actual status for your schedule and for actual timing. In other words, it is a convenient overview of the schedule as planned and as executed, but you may need more. The chart does not show how a delay during one phase affects the completion of a subsequent phase. One of the most effective steps you can take as project manager is to work to spot problems before they occur and counteract them before a delay results. This requires that you check regularly with team members to make sure that upcoming schedules remain practical and possible.

■ *The chart does not coordinate resources and networking requirements needed at critical phases of the schedule.* Many projects can proceed only when forms, documents, reports, outside help, and other outcomes are developed by the team or supplied by someone else. Some projects involve the development of basic forms, for example, to be used in a new procedure. It is possible that subsequent phases will not be able to begin until a single outcome is produced in the current phase. This is critical to your schedule. A delay brings the entire project to a complete halt in such cases. Identify the outcomes that are needed throughout the project to keep phases moving, and step in at those points to make sure your team members are on course.

■ *It does not show degrees of completion for each phase.* The Gantt chart is not practical for tracking completion progress within each phase. Because it is designed for overall tracking, you need to devise a method for keeping each phase on course, too. For especially complex phases or those requiring greater team participation and time, you may need to institute additional tracking methods, abbreviated charting, or direct participation and supervision. Once delays occur, it is too late to prevent them. However, if you monitor phases while they are progressing, you can spot and avoid emerging trends. Being aware of where the weak links and critical points exist will help you to keep on track.

· · · · · · · · · · ·

The Gantt chart is a useful tool for monitoring the big picture, working out modifications with your team, and keeping overall goals in sight. For more detailed monitoring, you need to be involved directly with team members and use more advanced techniques. The next chapter deals with these methods.

WORK PROJECT

1. Explain three or more points concerning delays in project phases and how they affect the final deadline and your management task.

2. You have been appointed as manager of a newly formed department. One of your first projects is to develop a one-year budget. You have defined the following phases. Which of these phases can be executed concurrently and which must be done consecutively?

Phase	Description
1	Identify assumptions for each expense category.
2	Develop initial budgets for each expense.
3	Cross-reference the budget summary to assumption worksheets.
4	Submit your initial budget for review.
5	Enter revisions.

6	Revise assumptions worksheets.
7	Prepare the final departmental budget.
8	Submit the final budget report.

3. Explain three or more possible ways to eliminate delays you might encounter during your project.

7

Flowcharting for Project Control

One machine can do the work of fifty ordinary men.
No machine can do the work of one extraordinary man.

—ELBERT HUBBARD—

"I'm tracking my project with a method used by the government for a submarine development program," one manager told another. "And now I can really identify with the Navy."

"Why, because it helps you keep your project on schedule?" the other one asked.

"No, because I'm having trouble keeping my head above water."

If you have a lot of time, you can develop and use a complex scheduling system to control your project. However, if you are facing the crunch most project managers face, you're continually battling to stay on schedule or just to catch up. The secret is to find an effective method you can put into play quickly that also gives you the daily information you need to control the schedule effectively. Remember, too, that no system can replace your personal effort and communication with team members; systems are only tools that you put into use.

The advantage of the Gantt chart is that you can put it together quickly. If properly tracked, your schedule can be controlled through Gantt chart monitoring overall as well as by specific phase.

The disadvantage of the Gantt chart is that it does not help you identify the weak links in your process, points where information passes from one person to another, where outside resources convey information to or receive information from your team, and where an action cannot be taken until someone else completes a preceding action. A Gantt chart only shows you when a project phase begins and ends and how actual times compare to the schedule. Your network—the actual communication and conveyance of information between core team members and other resources—can be tracked only with a more elaborate system.

Guidelines for Project Control

Any control procedure has to balance effectiveness with efficiency; this is not always easy. Your project is intended to move along at a healthy pace, with phases completed on time and within budget. That itself is a sign of effective leadership and control on your part. However, although effective control looks easy from the outside, it requires careful planning and leadership. Some guidelines to remember:

    1. *Define the criteria for the completion of each phase.* A lot of focus is placed on phases and their completion. This is important, of course, but what are your *criteria* for completion? Define successful completion for each of your phases. For example, if a phase involves designing an improved process, is it really an improvement? Is it faster, easier, better controlled? How do you know the project is moving in a positive direction? Your overall project goal may be clearly defined, but each phase should also be subjected to this standard.

    2. *Execute controls in manageable units.* Control is a concept that often cannot be achieved because the overall demand is overwhelming. Just as you read a book one chapter at a time, control has to be broken down into digestible, smaller units. You do not expect to accomplish all of your control steps in a single effort, so define the overall control expectation with a series of phase-specific steps. This makes the job easier and success much more likely.

3. _Hold regular (but short) meetings to check project status and to update everyone._ Meetings can kill any project, so they have to be kept brief and effective. Control cannot take place in a project manager's efforts alone; the whole team has to be involved. Whether you hold special meetings just to go over progress in control-related areas or incorporate this idea as an agenda item in your periodic team meetings, it is essential to spend time reviewing and planning the _control_ aspects of the process.

4. _Build in monitoring systems during phases._ As you design changes to processes, build in the control elements and ways to monitor them. Just as accountants have many rituals designed to ensure accuracy and protect liquid assets, every project manager needs to develop easily applied but effective methods for building red flags into the project. These will take on characteristics depending on the kind of project, work environment, and the project itself, but including a monitoring system is one of the most important forms of project control.

5. _Build control into the quality aspect of the project._ Control and quality are really not separate efforts. It is a mistake to attempt to break projects out into three different areas of work: process (input through output), quality (reduction of defects), and control (budgeting and scheduling, labor oversight, reduction of losses from theft or carelessness, for example). It's really one overall chain of events and the process, quality, and control issues are attributes of the whole effort. Your project is going to be more effective and successful when you merge these elements into one, single value chain (see Chapter 9).

6. _Anticipate problems to avoid them._ Control cannot be only a responsive matter. If you take steps to correct problems only after they occur, you miss the opportunity to prevent the same problems in the first place. Remember, too, that many problems are expensive in terms of profit and loss, customer relations, branding, and morale, to name a few areas. The whole concept of risk management recognizes the need not only to fix problems after they occur, but also to mitigate loss or prevent it altogether through farsighted control measures. Control based on avoiding loss may be the most valuable form, even though its dollar benefit is invisible. You never know how much money loss you *prevent* because the loss doesn't occur.

7. ***Communicate expectations, and then verify results.*** Leadership in your project is based largely on how your team is led. If you are able to express your specific expectations, you have every right also to get results; by the same logic, if you do not communicate your expectations, you have no right to the results you want. So if you don't make a specific goal about where you want to go, you have no way of knowing how well your team is performing. Of course, the mere communication of your expectations is only the first part of the two-part task. You also need to track progress and monitor results.

8. ***Use consistency to create a predictable control environment.*** Good project managers are consistent. Find a good working method with your team, and consistently apply the same controls, including communication, verification, monitoring, follow-up, and revision. Your consistency gives team members a sense of predictability while ensuring everyone that you know how to lead. Inconsistent behavior grows from not planning a project at all, but consistency is the lifeline the team wants and needs.

9. ***Be aware of high priorities, and put your energy there.*** In deciding which kinds of controls are needed and how to create them, also be constantly aware of priorities. Some controls are going to be quite urgent, whereas others are minor and can be deferred or delegated. For example, discovering that products are being shipped with defects is a critical priority, and the problem has to be fixed immediately. Worker complaints about low-quality coffee in the lunchroom affect morale but are nowhere as important as the first issue. Setting priorities makes you effective and helps move the improvements in your project to successful completion.

10. ***Be prepared for the unexpected, and move quickly to adjust.*** You can rely on one thing with certainty: You are going to face

unexpected problems during the course of your project. This is why no budget or schedule is ever final. Either has to be revised constantly. The normal chaos in this environment is going to challenge your leadership abilities, but as long as you are prepared to move quickly and adjust to unexpected problems, you will be able to steer the project to a successful, on-time, within-budget completion.

Listing Out the Phases

In Chapter 6, we used an example of an eight-phase project for improving procedures in a processing department. In that example, phases were broken down and listed in order of precedence. This is the first step in developing a definition of your project network; however, a problem may arise when you attempt to distinguish between an "event" and an "activity."

An activity is the step (or steps) involved at each phase. An event is the result (e.g., completion of a report) or some other necessary step (e.g., receipt of information from another team member).

As a general rule, an activity occurs during a phase and an event is what comes from the combined activities. The event commonly is a requirement before a subsequent phase can proceed.

Why are these definitions important? They point out a common flaw in the way that processes move along. If you make use of a flowchart to define a process, you will draw a series of boxes or circles that are joined together with lines. The tendency is to use boxes to describe activities, so the lines become nothing more than connectors between a series of sequential activities. How do you define time requirements in such a flowchart? You and your team can become confused if activities reside within the flowchart's boxes but time estimates are tracked on the lines. It is more accurate and easier to track processes when you use one of three alternate methods:

1. Writing events (i.e., the end results of phases) within boxes and using the lines in between to describe activities and the time required for those activities

Beyond Activities and Events—Interactions

Some additional definitions, while not essential to the listing of phases, also help to explain differences in how projects proceed. These relate to the three types of interactions that your core team experiences:

■ *Mandatory dependencies.* These are the requirements of a project. For example, a project involving revised departmental procedures includes mandatory dependencies on the work requirements for each employee in the department. These dependencies also are referred to as hard logic.

■ *Discretionary dependencies.* These are interactions left to team members. Whenever a team member has choices in how to proceed, that individual may rely on a particular approach or sequence to a problem, for example. Discretionary dependencies also are called soft logic.

■ *External dependencies.* These refer to any relationship between your core team and an outside resource, such as another department or division, a vendor, or a consultant, for example.

2. Isolating activities in the boxes with events written below in a separate box, then using the lines to describe the time requirements for activities

3. Writing activities in boxes with events listed below, and tracking time on a separate line

The first method is appropriate for large-scale and exceptionally complex projects. The second method enables you to track activities and time, the critical requirement for scheduling control, and to isolate and identify activities falling outside of that process flow. The third method can prove to be the most practical for smaller projects in terms of time and steps.

For any scheduling system more involved than the Gantt chart, begin by organizing phases in a logical sequence and by task or subtask within each phase. Your purpose should be to identify the precise sequence of activities and events and to recognize when the first draft includes out-of-sequence tasking. For especially complex phases, you may need to map out two or more events that come up at the same time.

Work Breakdown Structures

Work Breakdown Structure (*WBS*) is an organizational method for scheduling control. This method encompasses both outlines and graphs as a means for controlling your project schedule; you may need to develop and use both, or build flowcharts from a carefully constructed WBS in outline form.

The purpose in using WBS is to make sure that your schedule includes everything you are going to need to execute your project. It organizes your schedule by finding steps you may otherwise skip or overlook. There are important distinctions between WBS and the schedule itself. WBS is a tool you employ to make sure the schedule is comprehensive, that proposed phases are placed in the logical sequence, and that team assignments are given out logically, evenly, and based on required skills.

A good way to understand how WBS works is to see how it helps to create a powerful schedule. WBS lists tasks, and in the scheduling phase you determine their sequence; the same is true for task assignments. So given these distinctions, it makes the most sense to start out with WBS in outline sequence and then build a flowchart. As long as the WBS outline includes all known tasks and processes, the flowchart will determine (a) the logical sequence of work, (b) the proper team member or members to execute the work, and, most important of all, (c) the interdependencies of team members to one another and to stakeholders outside the team.

The use of a WBS outline to create a network diagram of the project or a finely detailed flowchart makes scheduling comprehensive and inclusive by cutting down on the chances that important phases will be left out. A common reason for scheduling problems is the discovery that work cannot proceed as originally planned because an important step was overlooked when the schedule was first created. WBS ensures that your original schedule will not be missing any steps.

Consider this example: You test a new procedure for two weeks. During the test, you compare outcomes with the old system four times and make any needed adjustments in the new procedures. In this case, the phase is broken down and identified by four separate events within the phase, one for each time the two systems' results are compared.

Organizing a project in this way is called WBS, and it can be achieved through either of two formats—the outline format or the tabular format.

The Outline Format

In the outline format, each phase is listed as a major heading and details are listed as subheadings. This format offers several advantages:

■ *You can identify responsibilities by team members.* On the outline itself, each task or series of tasks is first broken down by description. Once you are satisfied with the outline, you can assign team members to a task or series of tasks. If one team member will have primary responsibility and others will assist, this should be indicated as well. Thus, starting out with a rather simple outline, the entire project can be expanded into a nicely detailed summary of phases, steps, and responsibilities.

■ *You can control time in considerable detail.* The time estimate for each phase can be specified, and subroutines can be broken out in terms of hours or days estimated for completion. With the outline completed, you can then map out time requirements and constraints. The time element is a further elaboration of the sequence outline.

■ *You can look for weak links in the procedure where your involvement is required to keep the process moving along on schedule.* Controlling and managing weak links—points where work passes from one person or group to another or where one event has to be completed before another can begin—is the key to schedule control. Your outline can be used to highlight those critical points.

Achieving complete control over the schedule is the benefit to mapping out the schedule in complete detail. However, knowing where the weak links occur is only the first step in controlling them. You need to take two additional steps: bringing weak links to the attention of the team members who are involved in the work, and following up and monitoring the weak link itself to ensure that the process does not break down.

Also remember that team members on either side of the weak link (i.e., those passing along the work and those receiving it) can contribute to the breakdown of your schedule. To keep things moving along, you need the work completed and delivered, and you also need the receiving side to go into action right away.

Using the example project introduced in Chapter 5—the revision of current procedures in the accounts payable department—the outline format looks like this:

Project: Procedure Revisions
1.0 Document current procedures
      1.1 Interview employees
      1.2 Review documentation
      1.3 Update documentation
2.0 Prepare procedure flowcharts
      2.1 Identify workflow
      2.2 Coordinate work between employees
      2.3 Review flowcharts
      2.4 Adjust workflow
3.0 Summarize paper flow
      3.1 Prepare final workflow
      3.2 Identify sources
      3.3 Identify destinations
      3.4 List department reports
4.0 List problem areas and solutions
      4.1 List inefficient areas

4.2 Identify weak links

4.3 List possible solutions

4.4 Summarize solution ideas

5.0 Develop improved procedures

   5.1 Prepare flowcharts

   5.2 Develop narratives

6.0 Track sample transactions for one week under existing procedures

   6.1 Identify test area

   6.2 Track daily totals

   6.3 Summarize data

   6.4 Prepare summary report

7.0 Track sample transactions for two weeks under proposed procedures

   7.1 Isolate daily test area

   7.2 Process information

   7.3 Summarize data

   7.4 Compare to totals under old system

   7.5 Prepare comparison report

   7.6 Adjust new system as needed

8.0 Prepare and deliver final report

   8.1 Explain problem/solution

   8.2 Summarize test data

The Tabular Format

The second WBS method is the tabular, or organizational, format. The same information is arranged from top to bottom, with each phase broken down much like an organization chart, as shown in Figure 7-1.

Either the outline or tabular method can be employed. The outline format provides more flexibility for adding time and responsibility details, so the decision to use one method or the other should depend on the project's complexity and the size of your core team. Once you have completed the definitions in the WBS system, you can next prepare a diagram and time requirements in a visual format.

Figure 7-1. Tabular format.

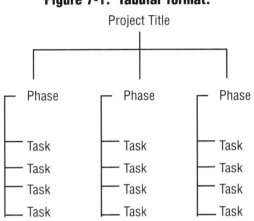

CPM and PERT Methods

Between 1956 and 1958, two scheduling control systems came into popular use. These are called Critical Path Method (CPM) and Program Evaluation and Review Technique (PERT). Both of these systems originally were designed to track time in projects involving concurrent activity and to monitor and control expenditures of time. Since their introduction, CPM and PERT have been expanded for use in many project applications, including budgeting, resource management, process definition, and quality control. When the two systems are combined and used together, the process is referred to as a PERT/CPM network.

In the most technical of uses, both CPM and PERT are used to analyze time use on a mathematical model. CPM provides modeling for phase start and end dates with the intention of identifying the float, or that amount of time that can be absorbed in later phases to offset time overruns in earlier ones. PERT is employed to show weighted averaging of phase time estimates and is not used as commonly as CPM.

While mathematical modeling provides some value to the highly technical project and a certain level of control to the project manager (particularly in engineering and similar environments), CPM and PERT can be used effectively purely for visual aid modeling. Leaving the mathematical analysis and weighted averaging of time studies behind, virtually any project manager can employ the techniques of these tools for visual control of any project. In fact, too much emphasis on purely mathematical modeling can take away time for hands-on management and supervision, and tends to move the project manager out of touch with the team.

A practical application for CPM involves using the visual representation of a project and its phases to calculate the maximum time in which projects can be completed, given overall deadlines. CPM can help you to identify points at which time segments can be moved around and time overruns can be absorbed without missing a final deadline. In CPM, concurrent activities are also called "parallel" tasks, and those activities that cannot begin until a previous activity has been completed are called "dependent" activities.

By mapping out the parallel and dependent activities in a model of the project, you can identify a pattern for how the job could progress. You can discover avenues for parallel activities that could save significant time throughout the project by identifying workflow with the use of CPM. The process of developing CPM often begins by organizing phases and developing a schedule using the Gantt chart. That information can then be converted to a CPM chart such as the one shown in Figure 7-2.

Figure 7-2 is a network diagram employing CPM principles. It shows the critical junctures and activities by numbers, each of which is circled. The time requirements to move from one activity to another are represented by the number of days estimated between activities (or phases). These are the numbers above or below lines joining the circled phases. Note that the concurrent, or parallel, activities are represented by a split in the critical path, as seen between the activities numbered 3 and 6 and again between 6 and 9 in the diagram.

Figure 7-2. CPM diagram.

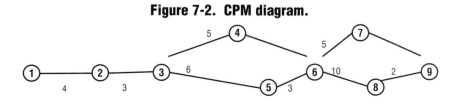

When CPM is used to schedule and track time alone, it still involves several separate factors: minimum and maximum time required, phase and project-to-date time expended, and earliest possible start and finish times. Procedures can be employed to track and calculate these times, and to isolate the floats available to you as project manager. Thus, CPM graphs can be used to present a combined best case and worst case, as well as identify potential floats that can be used to absorb unfavorable time variances.

As useful as the visual model of CPM is for large and complex projects, it may be too time-consuming to monitor manually and perhaps overly complex for smaller, shorter-term projects.

Automated Project Management Systems

Project management, like so many other business applications, lends itself well to automation. As long as you can put software to work quickly and don't have to spend excessive time working through software limitations, duties such as schedule control—especially where graphics are employed—can be made quick and efficient.

Automation is suitable whenever you are spending too much time maintaining a monitoring system. In other words, if your oversight duties remove you from the equally important routines that help you stay in touch with team members, then they are counterproductive and not efficient. If you need to manage a large body of project-related scheduling information, software makes more sense than trying to operate a system by hand. The best kind of software program is one that lets you, as project manager, input and review information without having to wait for someone else to process it for you. You'll also want to review how well graphics can be created and displayed in available software packages (see the sidebar "Charting Features of Scheduling Software"). A list of websites of vendors of scheduling software is offered in Chapter 6.

The decision to employ software as part of your project management duties depends on how many projects you are assigned. If you deal with isolated projects occasionally, it will be difficult to justify the cost of a suitable, versatile program. However, if project management

Charting Features of Scheduling Software

Many specialized scheduling programs allow you to construct graphic representations such as CPM, PERT, and Gantt charts. These include:

Project Kickstart	www.projectkickstart.com
SmartDraw	www.smartdraw.com
Task Manager	www.taskmanagementsoft.com
Primavera P6	www.primavera.com
Business Process Manager	www.planview.com

is a regular part of your duties, you may convince management that an investment in effective software will save time and money and assist you in delivering project outcomes on time.

Be sure that the software you consider purchasing is truly designed for project management—specifically that it provides you with scheduling and budget control features that you need. Some "project management" software packages are, in effect, nothing more than time management programs. Address files, e-mail notification and control, appointment reminders, and basic graphing capabilities are not worth the extra investment—not only because you probably have these features available to you as part of your operating system, but also because they provide no real value to justify the extra cost.

Other Resources

Check shareware and freeware sources to find flowcharting software online. One website worth reviewing is www.smartdraw2.com.

You may also be able to modify your existing graphics routines to create your own Gantt chart and schedule, budget, and other project-related controls. However, before automating by purchasing software, or modifying existing software in your operating system, be sure you take the following preliminary steps:

1. *Solve the problem of management over projects first.* Many of the difficulties you encounter in your role as project manager have to do with issues you cannot resolve through automation. These include human relations, time and budget estimation, and outside obstacles—in other words, exceptions to the way that processes should operate. You need to first master these management-related problems through experience, intuition, and knowledge. Automation is no replacement for good old-fashioned management.

2. *Identify recurring processes that are best handled through automation.* Within the project management realm, certain recurring tasks can be automated—just as certain of your departmental routines may be appropriate for automation. Because by their nature projects deal more with exceptions than with routines, you need to find software flexible enough to serve you in the ways you need. Beyond that, you will need to deal with nonroutine problems in nonroutine ways.

3. *Automate for efficiency of processing, and not to replace your direct involvement with your core team.* It is a mistake to believe that even the best software program can replace the need for direct management. The two have nothing in common. Never forget the need for direct and regular contact with team members.

4. *Don't confuse project objectives with automation objectives.* Another common problem is to let the underlying objectives of the project slide and become replaced with automation itself. The purpose of software is to give you the tools to manage information, arrange and report it in useful formats, and overcome paperwork and the time it wastes. Always keep the program and your objectives in mind.

5. *Don't change your procedures to fit a program's limitations.* A problem with software is that it might be designed for a particular type of project, and that won't always be a good fit for your work. When you end up with software that is not a good fit for your procedures, remember that the project should come first. Don't change the way you want to process work to fit with the design of the program.

6. *Develop a practical and efficient system for managing your projects manually.* First, overcome the problems associated with project management—as a facet of your management and leadership abilities rather than as routine-based processing methods. Next, look for ways to increase efficiency, save time, and improve communication. First comes your system for leading the team; only when that's under control should you concentrate on procedural ideas.

The most effective method for controlling a project with time constraints in mind involves the use of informative graphics, a well-thought-out schedule, and cooperation from your core team. Lacking those advantages, even the most expensive and sophisticated software will not help. Remember, the WBS, Gantt, and CPM techniques are graphic modeling provisions in software, or they are manual tools you can devise by hand. The software you select should make the use of those tools more efficient, rather than replace them with something better. You cannot expect software to take your place; its purpose is to improve your use of time and help with the communication of ideas between yourself and core team members.

Setting Your Flowcharting Rules

The essential tool for project management is the flowchart. However, to make your flowchart truly useful, you need to list much more than just activities and sequence. You also need to identify the important elements of responsibility by team member, time controls, events (e.g., reports, forms, information supplied from the outside), and coordination of every process within phases of the project.

In other words, the Gantt and CPM forms are useful, but they do not always go far enough. To make your project flowchart most useful, you have to expand beyond Gantt and CPM and also move away from traditional vertical flowcharting. You need to develop a series of rules to help in the construction of flowcharts. These rules are:

■ *Always use the precedence method.* To establish the correct sequence of activities and events, the entire project should be listed and flowcharted in the most logical format. This is most easily achieved beginning with a nicely detailed outline, such as the WBS format. Does each activity and event even fit according to what precedes it and what comes after it?

■ *Make sure the path of activities and events makes sense.* Your task in building the flowchart is simplified by recognizing that the lines connecting the boxes or circles are much more than connecting lines. The path of activities and events works only when it is arranged logically. Every action is generated by a preceding action or event and leads to a subsequent action or event. No one action should begin without a preceding one, and no action should ever lead to a dead end.

■ *Remember that an activity cannot occur until a preceding activity or event has been completed.* This rule assumes a direct connection between the current activity and the proceeding activity or event. Concurrent activities can also be under way and operated by different team members or groups. However, when scheduling your project, operate under the precedence constraint on each activity path.

■ *Plot, explain, and control concurrent events carefully.* Team members who are not used to working from network diagram flowcharts will be confused when the path splits off into two or more concurrent routes. As the flowchart begins to look like an electrical diagram, team members will find it difficult to follow the logic. Thus, plan each path carefully and ensure that the steps make perfect sense. You will need to lead team members through the maze to ensure that the steps in the flowchart are followed completely.

■ *Exercise control over weak links, as this is the key to successful project management.* More than anything else, the flowchart helps you to identify the weak links in the process. If errors and delays are going to occur, they probably will occur at these linking points— where work passes from one person or group to another. By knowing when and where these points occur, you can anticipate and prevent schedule delays that most often characterize projects. As the result of taking greater care over weak links, you provide the most effective form of scheduling control.

▧ *Make flowchart decision steps with great care, to avoid confusion.* A simple flowchart is not confusing; one step follows another. However, you will encounter decision points where the flowchart breaks into two or more segments, based on the complexity of the decision. A yes or no decision has two possible paths and subsequent steps; more complex decisions will involve more than two possible paths. Accompany decision points with narrative sections that offer additional explanation of actions for the team member who is affected by the outcome. Work closely with team members who will exercise the decision to proceed beyond that point, to ensure that the right path is taken.

· · · · · · · · · · ·

The next chapter shows how to combine all of the elements of project management and put the precedence method into action in order to provide yourself and your core team with the best tool possible: a working flowchart.

WORK PROJECT

1. Describe three benefits of organizing your schedule using Work Breakdown Structure (WBS) in outline form.

2. List and explain the guidelines for automating project management.

3. List and explain at least three rules for flowcharting.

Designing the Project Flowchart

*I have made good judgments in the past. I have made
good judgments in the future.*

—DAN QUAYLE—

"I gave up on flowcharting after trying it for a while," the manager
stated. "It was just too complicated."

"What do you mean?" the employee asked. "I thought flowcharting was supposed to help keep to a schedule."

"We finished on time. But instead of coming out with the result I
expected, we built a radio."

A visual summary of your project is essential for schedule control and
work assignments. Your project management function works best
when you think of it in terms of visual control features. Thus, your goal
is to come up with an effective flowcharting method, one that is more
than just a procedure. It has to be easy to work with and modify when
necessary. Too often, flowcharting itself becomes a useless procedure

that, once done, adds little or nothing to the actual process of running the project.

The Gantt chart helps you to identify the sequence of activities and events. That is a good starting point and helps in the identification of the initial schedule. Considering that there is much more to controlling your project, you need to move beyond the initial charting and develop a flowchart that allows you to track several activities at the same time: scheduling, work assignment, weak link identification, beginning and ending dates for phases, and event outcomes.

A project is likely to involve complex interactions among members of your core team and between the core team and outside resources. In most projects, the level of interactions will accelerate as the project moves into the midrange and end phases, so control at those points becomes critical. At those times, more elaborate and detailed flow-charting is called for. To be practical, you need to stick with the prece-dence method while designing a visual procedure that is effective for coordinating the efforts of many team members and outside resources, often operating on two or more paths within the project. You have to act in the role of coordinator and supervisor. If any one path of activity is delayed, it will affect the other paths and all future phases, as well as the final deadline.

Imagine how difficult a task you face with ten, fifteen, or more core team members when five or six phases are under way at the same time. A well-designed flowchart helps you to keep track of all the work going forth at the same time without having to directly supervise each and every step. The flowchart helps you to keep an eye on the future while helping several subteams continue along their paths. In this respect, the project manager operates like a conductor leading a large orches-tra. He cannot be in all sections of the orchestra at the same time and cannot take over and play instruments himself; he has to stand in the leadership position and follow the score. Just as the score reminds the conductor what each and every instrument and section needs to do, the flowchart shows the project manager how to keep all sections to-gether, work harmoniously, and conclude the project in a timely manner.

The goal of bringing a complex project to a timely conclusion requires that you keep a close eye on responsibility for each activity within each phase. One problem with the Gantt chart is that it is not set up to define responsibilities among team members, nor does it show how to coordinate those responsibilities when multiple tasks are proceeding together. The emphasis is on sequence and time alone. An alternative, the network diagram, provides you with all of the information you require and combines scheduling with assignments on one continuous form; it also identifies the precedence of activities and events, even when several are proceeding concurrently.

Activity and Event Sequences

Think of the flowchart as a visual procedural summary for your project. Rather than working from a narrative listing of duties and responsibilities, the flowchart identifies activities and events in a simple visual manner. You can achieve a lot of detail with simple square or rectangular boxes (representing activities and events) and lines (representing precedence and workflow).

Most people are familiar with the vertical flowchart. This design is natural since we write narratives from top to bottom, and the origin of flowcharting is an attempt to create a visual representation of workflow in the same manner. The starting point is at the top and the end is at the bottom. Any decision points loop back to a previous step; any concurrent activities call for dividing the flow into sequences shown left to right. The vertical flowchart works quite well when one individual executes all steps and makes all decisions, and when one activity follows another with a limited number of decisions or concurrent paths. However, most projects involve several people, many concurrent paths, and complex decision-making points.

A useful and practical working document should be based on precedence. However, individual team members will be less concerned with the big picture (in other words, what other individuals or team groups are doing) and more concerned with their routines. Thus, their interests are with the immediate phase and its tasks.

A good starting point is to identify the attributes of events that have to occur in your project. The final outcome is only the last event.

Chances are, many other events will be required as well. It is necessary to carefully define the kinds of interactions you will encounter during the course of a project. This effort helps you to recognize weak links, improve interteam communications, and develop a flowchart that can serve as a working document to guide you and your team through what may be a complex project maze. In defining activities and events, several assumptions can be made:

    ■ ***Some events have predetermined sequences.*** An event has to be completed before subsequent activities can begin. (This is the basic rule under the precedence method.) A future activity, then, requires completion of a prior action. This situation is called a *singular* effort, and it is the simplest version of work progress. If you are solely responsible for a phase, you can break it down into a series of singular activities and events.

    ■ ***Some events depend on multiple activities.*** Some events do not occur after the completion of a singular activity. For example, your next step may require completion of the current step plus completion of another activity by a second team member. This is one of the weak links where delays can occur—when one person's work progress depends on the timely completion of work by someone else. When two or more people work to finish activities, both of which are required for the event, it is called a *joint* effort.

    ■ ***Activities and events can take place apart from each other.*** Some events can occur only after someone else has completed a separate activity. This is another weak link that invites delay in your schedule. A team member responsible for the event can proceed only after someone else has completed a prior activity. This situation is called a *dependent* effort.

    The three types of sequences are illustrated in Figure 8-1. Note that the singular effort occurs on one horizontal line, indicating that one team member is responsible for the activities and the event. Joint and dependent efforts are split into more than one line because more than one person is involved in the workflow.

Figure 8-1. Sequences of activities and events.

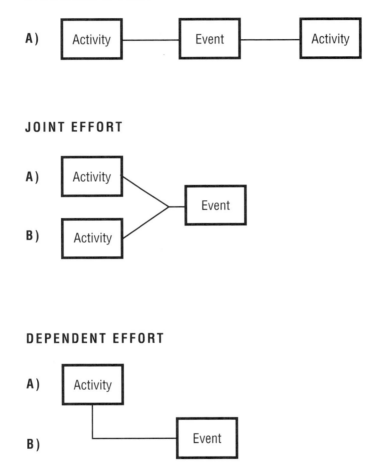

SINGULAR EFFORT

JOINT EFFORT

DEPENDENT EFFORT

These are important distinctions, and being aware of the differences helps keep your project on schedule. The distinctions also help your core team members to understand their role and the big picture, avoiding the all too common confusion that accompanies projects. In other words, good definition helps avoid chaos.

Weak links can include problems on several different levels of your project. Weak links can occur when passing information from one core team member to another; when processing toward a common event involves multiple paths; and when the team cannot proceed until an outside resource acts in some way.

The Vertical Flowchart and Its Limitations

When asked to prepare a flowchart, most people go immediately to the vertical format. This is natural and to be expected, and it's even appropriate for relatively simple processes. Using the example from Chapter 6, where the project involves revising accounts payable procedures and testing them, the vertical flowchart can be prepared quickly from an outline such as this one:

Phase	Description
1	Document procedures.
2	Prepare flowcharts.
3	Summarize paper flow.
4	Describe problems and solutions.
5	Design improved procedures.
6	Track the old system for one week.
7	Track the new system for two weeks.
8	Prepare the final report.

Recalling that phases 3 and 4 and phases 6 and 7 are executed concurrently, a vertical flowchart can be prepared, as shown in Figure 8-2.

While this format presents the steps directly and in the proper sequence, the vertical flowchart has several flaws. They are relatively minor for a simple project such as the one in the example, but when they are carried over to a more complex project, the flaws present significant management problems. These flaws are:

■ *The flowchart does not show time requirements for each phase.* All it shows is the sequence of activities. Thus, to watch time as well as sequence, you would need both a vertical flowchart and a Gantt chart.

■ *The flowchart does not let you see the division of responsibilities.* Like the Gantt chart, this flowchart does not give you a break-

Figure 8-2. Vertical flowchart.

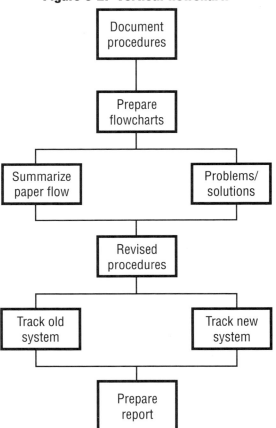

down by team member or subgroup. Even with a vertical flowchart and a Gantt chart, this essential element is lacking.

■ *The vertical flowchart does not show concurrent activities in adequate detail.* Breaking out the top-to-bottom sequencing is a first step, but it does not provide you with a combined activity and time picture of what needs to occur.

For effective scheduling control, the vertical flowchart has no real value. It is just a visual form of the outline, expressed in boxes and lines rather than as a list. However, it is useful as a preliminary step toward developing a more practical flowchart: the horizontal network diagram, also called the Precedence Diagramming Method (PDM).

The Horizontal Network Diagram and Its Advantages

Some project managers view horizontal flowcharting as nothing more than an elaboration of the Critical Path Method (discussed in Chapter 6) for managing time and resources. However, it is much more. The practical applications of the horizontal network diagram enable you to express even the most complex project in a concise, visual format. The diagram serves not only as an effective and practical control mechanism, but also as a training tool. The properly developed horizontal network diagram is the key to managing even the most complex project, training and orienting your core team, and expressing schedule and work-sharing ideas.

To develop the horizontal flowchart, you should start out with a vertical flowchart as a way to communicate a Work Breakdown Structure (WBS) outline, if only to make sure that your steps take place in a logical sequence. For complex projects with many phases, a large core team, and many concurrent paths, the real order of execution will not be obvious from a vertical flowchart alone. Any sequencing problems will be discovered only when you begin work, and at that time the need to redefine the sequence is likely to throw your schedule into disarray. It will also be confusing to team members. The advantage to the horizontal network diagram is that it can be developed in advance while providing you with all of the elements you require.

Using the activity steps shown in the vertical flowchart, you can add more information when you map out the project horizontally. However, activity sequence is only the skeleton for the body of your schedule control system. To round it out, you also need to identify and track:

■ Deadlines for each phase

■ Time requirements and constraints for each step

■ Individual team members or subgroups who will execute each phase

▨ Weak links (i.e., where effort involves two or more people or groups)

▨ Flow of work from activity to activity, leading to events

▨ Definition of events that will be produced throughout the project

All of these features can be incorporated into the horizontal flowchart without making it overly complex and without losing the simplicity that makes flowcharting effective. Individual team members and subgroups can follow their own requirements and see how they interact with other team members. The advantages of the horizontal flowchart include:

▨ *It shows interaction between team members.* Project activities and events do not occur in isolation. If they did, each team member would be able to execute a phase without the involvement of anyone else. The points where interaction occurs are the points you need to watch most closely, because you need to coordinate the efforts of the team and not just the work of each individual.

▨ *It establishes an exact sequence.* Attempts to flowchart without application of the precedence method invariably run into problems. Some projects wander from a set schedule because of confusion over the proper sequencing that is required; thus, a phase is held up because a necessary step was scheduled in the wrong place. The horizontal flowchart tracks sequence logically and easily, even when several paths are going on at the same time.

▨ *It draws attention to weak links.* Since precedence of activity may involve two or more core team members (not to mention outside resources), you need to guide the schedule through its weak links. The horizontal flowchart makes these links easy to spot, showing you where you need to concentrate your attention.

▨ *It breaks down areas of responsibility.* The horizontal flowchart shows all activities for each team member or subgroup. These activity areas are best described as areas of responsibility rather than simply tasks to be performed by individuals, departments, or teams. One person will not always be solely responsible for a range of tasks. Some areas of responsibility will be a single individual; others will be a subgroup or team within the project team; still others will be an entire department or an outside resource. The horizontal flowchart distinguishes specific areas of responsibility so that everyone can see with ease who does what, when it is done, and how work paths pass from one area to another.

■ *It shows concurrent activity flow.* Project managers are easily overwhelmed by the complexity of the process itself, notably when the process breaks down into several concurrent paths. For a complicated project, you may need to oversee a large number of different tasking paths at the same time. If you are not able to track each and every one, you lose touch with the overall progress of the project, and delays and confusion are usually the result. The horizontal flowchart is designed to manage any number of concurrent paths, including interaction between areas of responsibility.

■ *It ties actions to time controls.* The horizontal flowchart includes a timeline. This combines the best features of the Gantt chart and vertical flowchart together. When each activity and event is fit onto the timeline, you have a much better tool for managing the entire schedule.

■ *It lists reports, forms, and other documents—the "events" of each phase.* Your project probably includes the requirement of event outcomes. These can include interim and final reports; worksheets, forms, and other new documents; as well as information you receive from outside resources. The horizontal flowcharts include a complete listing of all documents generated by project team efforts.

■ *It aids in communication with your core team.* Schedule control doesn't take place in the project manager's office; it depends on team effort. The horizontal flowchart allows you to demonstrate to your team where problems are expected, how you plan to solve them, and how different activities occur at the same time. Most of all, the horizontal flowchart provides an excellent visual representation of the entire project, which benefits all team members.

■ *It allows you to detect and correct schedule variances.* As your project moves ahead, you will experience scheduling variances for any number of reasons. That isn't a problem. The real problem comes up when you don't have the information you need to correct the variances when they occur, or to take action to get the project back on schedule. The horizontal flowchart shows you where variances are likely to occur so that preventive measures can be taken. It also shows you where likely process times are so that you can absorb time delays. That means you have a chance to take corrective action, such as shifting duties, doubling up effort, or looking for ways to cut down on time requirements in future phases. The horizontal flowchart helps you study these questions and make informed decisions.

■ *It identifies alternatives.* The initial outline and schedule developed in the form of a Gantt chart or vertical flowchart are reasonable starting points. But when problems arise in the schedule or in core team workload, you must be able to move quickly and modify the original schedule. The horizontal flowchart helps to manage the flow of process information so that even the most complex paths can be modified to suit ever-changing situations.

Building the Network Diagram

The horizontal flowchart, or network diagram, is a left-to-right breakdown of each activity. An example of this format is shown in Figure 8-3.

Lines connect activity boxes, but only as a means of demonstrating the sequence of the process and divisions between areas of responsibility. Each box is a separate activity within the sequence and is limited to actions, with events (or results) listed beneath the process flow sections.

This format provides you with all of the scheduling and control features you need. If you look more carefully at the major features of the horizontal flowchart depicted in Figure 8-3, you'll see it also serves as a training tool for your core team. For example:

Figure 8-3. Network diagram format.

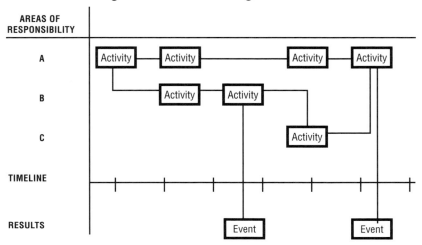

Areas of responsibility are described in the first column. Each one (A, B, and C in Figure 8-3) has its own left-to-right process flow so that members of that particular area can see without any trouble exactly what activities they will execute, when those activities occur, and how a work process comes to them, as well as where it goes.

Activities are shown in the order of execution. When a concurrent path is under way, two or more activity boxes appear, separated into areas of responsibility.

Events go on the "results" line. Events are separated from activities since the event is the result of completing the activity. This allows you to review all outcomes (e.g., reports, forms, worksheets) of the project, where they come from, and how they are developed.

Timeline identifies the time requirements for each activity. It can be the number of hours or days, depending on how you have organized your schedule and are tracking actual results. You may increase the use of the horizontal flowchart by including two time numbers: estimated time for completion above the line and the cumulative estimate on the bottom half of the line.

The network diagram containing all of these elements provides you with a management tool that removes any guesswork and relieves your having to refer to several sources (e.g., labor hours estimates, time estimate, and a Gantt chart). All of the important information for overseeing your project is contained in the one diagram.

When mapped out in this format, a project can require several pages. For example, if you employ twelve areas of responsibility and twenty-five separate phases, broken down into a hundred or more distinct activities, the network diagram will be long and complex. However, the information it provides will be far more useful than if it were compiled in any other format. In addition to serving as a useful management tool, the horizontal flowchart also provides a useful map for each core team member.

The complexity of the project does not present a problem; the network diagram format is suitable for even the most complex of projects. Because multiple concurrent activity paths can lead to confusion, both among team members and for the project manager, a system is needed to track everything at the same time. Using the network diagram provides that capability.

The network diagram is an efficient management tool when multiple concurrent phases are under way, notably when they also are interdependent. For example, one phase may have fifteen activities and another ten. But the second phase has two or three stopping points, awaiting information that develops out of the first phase. In this complex situation, the network diagram illustrates the requirements and helps coordinate the efforts between the groups working on each phase—while also allowing you to keep an eye on the timeline. The key here is in your ability to visualize not only the timing and interaction between two or more subgroups, but also to manage the weak links inherent in the interaction.

The network diagram is also a useful tool for phase review. At the end of each phase, you should ask yourself and your team members a series of questions:

  ▪ Have we completed the activities that need to be completed in order to create the events or to move forward to the next phase?

■ What weak links are we facing today or likely to encounter in the immediate future?

■ What actions should we take now to ensure that we stay on schedule?

■ What results do we need from outside resources? Can we make our requests early to prevent the possibility of delay?

■ Are we on schedule? If not, where can we make up the variance?

Your efforts will be concentrated on a small portion of the network diagram, specifically weak links and completion points. Upon ending one phase, the next phase should be taken up without pause. When you look over steps coming up in the next few days, weak links will be apparent. You may also need to anticipate periods of exceptionally heavy workflow activity and take preemptive action to ensure that core team members will be available to put in the hours needed. The ever-present timeline allows you to keep a complex project moving all the way through to final completion.

The diagram is constructed in a series of logical steps—beginning with the initial WBS, then creating a vertical outline (if you find that step to be necessary), and then, as a last step, placing the elements onto the horizontal flowchart, with activities moving left to right instead of top to bottom. It is important to go through this process efficiently because a lot of valuable time is consumed if your schedule design is too lengthy. It may be necessary to create a working flowchart with enough information to get the team moving, even though you may need to make changes as work progresses. You can work in one of three ways:

1. ***Build the network diagram on your own.*** You may find that the best use of time is to independently work through the steps required to develop a preliminary network diagram. Then call together the members of your core team, go through the whole process, and invite ideas for improvements or to correct obvious schedule errors.

2. ***Employ the entire team to build the network diagram.*** This is the most difficult approach. Committees do not act and they are not

efficient. However, if phases will involve highly specialized areas of responsibility, you may not know all the steps required for a particular segment of the workflow. Team participation may be a necessity. If so, try to make the process move quickly to avoid using up too much time that could be better spent executing phases.

3. _Use a small group._ As a compromise, consider asking only two or three team members to help build the network diagram. While committees are less efficient than individuals, a small committee is preferable to a large one. Upon completion of the draft, it can be presented to the full team for review and modification.

Applying the Network Diagram

Using the eight-step project example presented previously, how should the network diagram be presented? In practice, each and every activity will be isolated in its own activity box, assigned to the proper area of responsibility, and placed on the timeline. Thus, every team member will be aware of who does what, when it is to be completed, and what sequences are involved. However, for the purpose of illustrating this process, the eight steps in our sample project are listed by number. And rather than listing the titles of people in each area of responsibility, they are referred to (for illustrative purposes) as A, B, and C. The network diagram for this simplified project example is shown in Figure 8-4. The diagram has several noteworthy features that are worth commenting on:

■ **_Weak links are highly visible._** These occur in four places: between steps 2 and 4; steps 5 and 6; 6 and 7; and 7 and 8. On a Gantt chart or vertical flowchart, these weak links would not be identified. Only the network diagram reveals these potential problem points.

■ **_The solid lines represent primary activity steps; the broken lines represent secondary or supportive activity._** The broken lines help further define primary workflow while still separating out areas of responsibility.

Figure 8-4. Network diagram application.

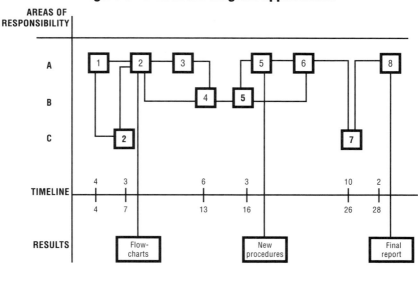

A = Accounts Payable Supervisor
B = Accounting Manager
C = Systems Analyst

■ *Activities and events are clearly distinguished.* Activities are shown in boxes placed in the process flow section, and events are broken out and separated below in the "results" section. This helps clarify the process for you and for core team members.

■ *The results section is nicely detailed.* The various items showing up as results show the interim and final outcomes of the project. For complex projects with numerous interim events, this is a very important and valuable feature.

■ *The timeline puts the process in a good scheduling perspective.* The timeline in Figure 8-4 shows each activity's schedule in terms of days (above the line) and the cumulative time schedule (below the line). In the example, the project should be completed within twenty-eight days.

Expanded Applications

This sample project involves a small team and a simplified number of phases. While these parameters aid in illustrating the horizontal flowchart, they probably won't apply to many of the projects you will manage. It is likely that you will work with more complex teams, many more activities and phases, and multiple instances of concurrent paths.

Three examples of projects where the network diagram is especially useful are those involving the development of new procedures, converting old systems or processes into new ones, and coordinating the efforts of many people or departments.

Example 1

You are working on a project to document all procedures within your department. Workflow includes interaction between department members as well as with other departments, both for receipt of information and delivery of reports. A narrative description would be difficult to explain to someone else because these interactions occur on many levels. At the same time, a description of each employee's actions would not provide a context for the work of the entire department.

Solution: A network diagram lists each employee's workflow as a horizontal flowchart, including not only each activity but also identifying the exchange of information and documents between other department members and outside departments. Each person's tasks can be tracked along their individual area of responsibility line; overall functions can be reviewed together, including identification of weak links, reports, and the timeline (which corresponds to your department's monthly cycle).

Example 2

Your company is undergoing full automation of several departments currently using outdated manual processes. Your project is to prepare complete documentation needed by systems analysts, showing each and every processing step; to identify input formats and fields and the type of information to be processed; to describe database requirements; and to define and design the desired results.

Solution: The department's processes, when reduced to a network diagram, can be identified quickly and separated into two activity groups: recurring routines, which are easily adapted to automated processes, and exceptional routines, which may not fit into the proposed automation scheme. Those activities treated as exceptions require a different type of procedural treatment. The network diagram will also identify input as well as output design requirements (e.g., forms, worksheets, or reports).

Example 3

You are designing a marketing tracking procedure. When it is finalized, several departments will use the procedures: marketing management, field offices, accounting, and marketing/sales support groups in various regions.

Solution: To best describe the procedures you are designing, a network diagram does the job well. A narrative description would be confusing, whereas anyone can review the horizontal workflow, get a handy overview of the whole process, and see their part in it.

. . . .

Besides providing you with a good management tool and a communication device, the network diagram improves feedback. Anyone working on the user end will quickly recognize gaps or flaws in the horizontal flowchart, and no doubt will be glad to let you know that your network diagram contains errors. That provides you with the information you need to fix the problem before it appears during actual execution and use.

Some projects require a written document as well as visual representations. Because people are not accustomed to complete visual help in matters such as internal procedures, the narrative supplement is required in many instances; it also helps to expand on the meaning that a visual representation provides. One drawback to any flowcharting method is that it does not provide the procedural background. It tends to show how work proceeds, but does not tell employees why they are going through the steps. That is the function of narrative support.

The next chapter explores how narrative sections can help expand the project flowchart and make it complete and effective for the people who will execute the tasks—either project team members or other employees.

WORK PROJECT

1. Explain the difference between an activity and an event in the following cases:
   a. Writing a report
   b. Receiving a report from another department and using it to develop statistical summaries as part of a project phase
   c. Summarizing sales activity information from four separate divisions and using that information to describe a reporting problem

2. Explain the flaws of vertical flowcharting and how those flaws are overcome by using a network diagram.

3. Explain why it is essential to identify weak links. How is a network diagram used to ensure continuing schedule control where weak links are involved?

Managing the Value Chain in the Project

Intractable problems are usually not intractable because there are no solutions, but because there are no solutions without severe side effects.

—LESTER C. THUROW—

"Why is management suddenly so interested in plumbing problems?" one manager asked another as they both read a memo from the vice president.

The second manager looked puzzled. Then he realized what the problem was. "No, you misunderstood. The memo says that we need to work on our *value* chain, not our *valve* chain."

The *value chain* is a concept defining levels of both quality control and process management. Just as the better known supply chain has to be carefully controlled to prevent process defects, the value chain also requires careful quality control–related overlays in preventive measures.

The supply chain describes how processes move from beginning to end. It includes descriptions of the responsible person or department at each step, and it shows how work flows from one step to another.

Supply chain is characterized by weak links, those specific times and places where defects are most likely to occur. In quality control processes such as Six Sigma, the definition and scope of a project are often defined in terms of weak links. Most analysis reveals that weak links occur whenever a process moves from one person or department to another. Once you identify these problem areas, likely solutions are much more easily quantified and reached. However, supply chain describes only the movement of process and does not discuss quality along the way. It is an action plan, not a quality-control plan. The study of supply chain is very useful in focusing on weak links and making sure that all steps have been examined. This is why a visual representation of supply chain is valuable, but it is most valuable when it also leads to a second discussion, focused on quality.

Apply the same logic used in the supply chain to the concept of quality, and the value chain can be monitored under the same kind of process. Once you merge supply chain and value chain, you complete the goal of (a) improving processes in terms of efficiency, (b) looking for weak links causing delays or defects, and (c) identifying how and where quality must be improved and focused to make the whole process better in terms of efficiency *and* quality.

Attributes of the Value Chain

The definition of a value chain is determined by the kind of project. If your project involves product manufacturing and the reduction of defects (the original quality control format for projects), then value chain is easily understood. For example, an auto manufacturer wants reduced defects on the assembly line. As noted, companies like Toyota revolutionized assembly line work by allowing anyone on the assembly line to bring the whole thing to a halt if a defect was found. This is where the supply chain crosses over to the value chain.

If your project is more service oriented, the same concepts apply but the appearance will be vastly different. For example, a process to improve internal controls or make processing more efficient is equally concerned with quality control, but the means by which this is achieved will vary considerably. Just as the auto assembly employee can bring the line to a halt upon recognizing a flaw created by a previous process, the most effective value chain allows for internal self-auditing and cross-auditing of the process. It does this not only to highlight defects, but to ensure that the output quality is of the highest level as well. The identification of flaws and defects—whether product or service re-lated—is the most important attribute of value chain management.

Attributes of this approach to a project define its success. These include:

1. *Value can be thought of as a form of quality, although the two are not always precisely the same.* In some respects, the cre-ation of value within the supply chain shares many attributes with qual-ity, but not always. For example, in a product assembly environment, preventing product defects creates value by reducing waste and speed-ing up processes. The end result is greater quality. However, in a ser-vice-oriented venue, value may exist simply because a process is made more efficient, thus reducing processing cost and time; but this does not mean the end result contains more quality. The distinction is im-portant because in those kinds of situations, there is an important goal: to create more value without a corresponding loss of quality. Greater value exists only when the same or better quality control is maintained.

2. *The value chain requires quality-control measures, but also a customer service outlook.* The value chain is closely associ-ated with the historical idea of customer service. If your project creates a better outcome for customers (better-quality product or service, im-proved responses to complaints, more focused marketing), then value chain is a quality control system. If your customer is an internal individ-ual or department, then the same outlook has to be applied to grant real value to your project, but this is beyond the scope of quality con-trol.

For example, an accounting department that processes payroll checks has the internal controls and processes in place to ensure accu-rate calculation of gross pay and deductions, but it still has problems with timing for the release of those paychecks if and when exceptions are presented (i.e., overtime calculations, variances in pay rates, or special and nonrecurring deductions). Even in fully automated systems, these typical kinds of exception-based processes become problems if processes are not flexible. So with quality control in place, the required safeguards are going to exist, but the value chain has to be designed so that, beyond quality control (in this example, involving the accuracy of calculations) must be balanced with the equally important expectation on the part of the customer (anyone receiving a paycheck) that payroll checks will be received on a timely basis and consistently.

3. *If you apply the same diligence to value as you do to the prevention of process-related defects and variances, then the entire supply chain works; without this value-based orientation, problems are inevitable.* In many projects, emphasis is placed on steps and phases alone, without adequate consideration of value. This focus on reducing defects and variances may have an unintended consequence. If the end result lacks actual value, changed processes may be less efficient and more expensive; even with improvements in the process, forgetting value often means that projects fail even when safeguards and process improvements are built into the system. This may also be reflected in the difficulty with maintaining changes and improvements after the project is over. When an element of value is incorporated into the new process, you still reduce the defects that were the original project target; you also improve value as an integrated part of the newly revised process. This augments the permanence of the changes.

4. *The effectiveness of the value chain often determines whether improvements to processes are permanent or not.* A real test of how effectively new processes work is the question of whether they remain in effect once the project team breaks up. In spite of what the theories in many Six Sigma and project management texts claim, the changes are not permanent just because a project changes the process. The key to ensuring that improvements are kept in place rests with the value chain. When the steps in a process are incorporated with the concept of value (customer service in addition to process integrity), those responsible for execution of each step are more likely to keep newly implemented procedures in place. Most employees, whether

working on product-related output or services, want to reduce defects, for two reasons. First, everyone wants high quality, as a matter of simply being effective on the job. Second, people realize over time that low-quality output inevitably means processes return and have to be fixed, resulting in more work for less result, and people usually do not want to have to do anything twice or spend more time and effort going over the same processes twice.

5. *Effective value chain naturally makes the whole process easier, not harder.* Some resistance to change has to be expected, and a project manager's greatest challenge may be to get others to go along with changes, even small ones. In fact, resistance to change often is not only a challenge; it may also be a stumbling block that can defeat the project before it is even implemented. The irony is that people resist change because they see it as a complication in their routine. With this in mind, one of the most important points to remember in the design of a project is this: An effective value chain reduces the workload and processing burden. The assumption that change and complication are indistinguishable is wrong, as long as value is built into the process.

For example, information technology (IT) has made some processes complex because a different set of risks come with the change. It has made everything much easier as well by removing the detail orientation of repetitive functions and routines. So much more data is processed much more quickly and with greater accuracy before IT was widely applied in work environments. The processing burden has been reduced even though some complications have arisen. Any process that includes a greater value element is going to simplify the whole process. Even when this simplification changes the risk structure and internal controls, it remains a simplification. Part of your project management challenge is going to be to demonstrate to the stakeholders and end users why change is actually an improvement in their processing lives. That is the real challenge.

Risk Management and the Value Chain

The value chain is specifically intended to reduce risks, prevent them, and anticipate possible future risks. On a large scale, catastrophic losses cannot be insured against or transferred, so steps have to be taken to mitigate the risks. For example, IT files can be duplicated off-site, the labor force can be diversified by location, and internal emergency drills can be put in place for natural disasters (notably in areas known to experience hurricanes, earthquakes, or tornadoes).

On a small scale—for example, as part of the structure of the project focused on relatively concentrated processing—a few basic risk management principles help to (a) reduce losses, (b) avoid variances and defects, whether product specific or service related, and (c) create greater overall quality (higher Sigma) by integrating quality into the value chain while creating a risk management approach.

Some essential risk management principles can help to incorporate value into the project and related processes. These include five specific points:

1. *Recognize that all processes contain risks.* No process can be designed completely risk free. Even if you mitigate, insure, and transfer all of the risks you can imagine, you still are exposed to the unimagined risk, to system failure, and even to intentional sabotage circumventing your controls. The best you can do is to anticipate as many known risks as possible and then take steps to avoid or reduce them. Safeguards like the use of safety glass, highly recognizable colors on steps, and self-locking ladders are good examples of small and simple ideas that reduce accidents. Apply the same principle to the entire process to address the reality that risk is universal.

2. *Plan for the worst-case scenario.* Many organizations have adopted a passive approach to risk, often citing budgetary limits for the decision. Although financial limitation is a reality, it is often not tied to the prioritization of risk. There are many risks a company simply cannot afford, and not every threat can be insured against or transferred to vendors and subsidiaries. Your plan within the project should be to anticipate the worst possible outcome. Knowing that you cannot do away with every possible risk, you can place control systems and safeguards at least to reduce the level of risk.

3. *Try to imagine risks that no one has even considered.* Many catastrophes occur because no one was able to imagine the threat. This has been one of the devastating lessons of 9/11. No one ever imagined an assault using commercial airliners, and as a consequence no one planned for it. On that day, first responders discovered, for example, that fire and police units could not communicate with each other because their equipment was not compatible. There was no plan in place, nor was there a policy, for deciding what kind of military response was to be made if additional planes were in the air and headed for targets. The list of ways that no one was prepared is long. The lesson can be applied in organizations as a factor in long-term, organizationwide planning. As a project manager, you can also improve your risk management skills by trying to imagine scenarios beyond the common and the usual.

4. *Match risk mitigation controls to the level of risk.* Prioritize your risk management decisions within the project to match the highest threats with the most extensive steps. In risk management, prioritizing is the only way to intelligently mitigate loss. You cannot plan for every conceivable risk, and, even if you could, the comprehensive program would be cost prohibitive. So a two-part approach to prioritizing is needed.

The first part is to evaluate a threat level, based on the likelihood of an event. For example, it is quite likely that a strike will disrupt manufacturing, transportation, and other phases of the supply chain; it is much less likely that a pandemic will close your offices and plants. So you would probably prioritize risk mitigation initiatives to reduce the impact of a strike (by creating additional inventory for essential products or diversifying supply sources, for example), and assign a lower priority to reacting to a pandemic.

The second part is to prioritize the cost element of mitigation and prevention. Steps like insuring against loss are part of this, but only a small part of the total response. Any risk that is both cost prohibitive and unlikely to occur will probably not be given high priority; those more likely to occur will be given higher priority, but limited to cost-effective measures.

These prioritizing steps are applied throughout the organization; but projects can also be subjected to the same kinds of analysis. The combined likelihood and cost associated with a threat are going to determine how you need to address risk management. Some projects are going to be chronically high risk. For example, in a manufacturing plant, the risk of accident is going to be quite high; in a clerical setting, it is quite low.

5. *Incorporate risk mitigation as a permanent part of the process.* As project manager, the challenge is not limited to identifying and preventing or mitigating risks. It extends to how you can incorporate risk management into the entire process, not as a function but as an integrated part of a newly developed process and as part of the control procedure itself. Many risk initiatives start out working brilliantly, but once management moves out of the picture, those mitigating steps are ignored or dropped. The safety devices come off, exact procedures are shortened, and internal controls are not taken seriously. By developing risk management processes as part of the process itself, it is more likely that the benefits will be made permanent.

How Value Is Incorporated into the Big Picture

One of the great advantages of Six Sigma is its two-part application. It is a quality control and project management system with a highly structured approach to fixing problems. It is also a cultural point of view. According to the philosophy of Six Sigma, everyone in the company, regardless of rank, is on the same organizational team. So widespread objectives, quality standards, and processing goals are at the base of every project organized under the Six Sigma ideal. Value itself becomes part of everything done in the organization, and projects are always based on the assumption that value is going to improve as a result of the project.

This ideal can simply be empty words, or it can serve as a new way to approach project challenges. The distinction relies on project leadership, organizational morale, the degree of team spirit (whether as part of Six Sigma or not), and a willingness to work together to reach clearly stated organizational goals.

Each of these deserves a closer look. As a project leader, it is not enough to ensure that team members respond to your directives or efficiently execute the steps you assign. So, although *project leadership* is an essential element, it is only the means by which additional steps can be put into action. A leader needs to understand the elements of leadership that define the difference between success and failure; having the authority to lead your team is necessary, but it does not mean you will succeed as a leader. True leaders need to inspire team members and motivate them to adopt the teamwide goals. Of course, those goals have to be expressed clearly to the team. If a team leader closely guards the real goals of the project, it is not reasonable to expect team members to actively participate in accomplishing those goals. Many project managers discover that a large part of their job is motivating members through the constant definition and clarification of team-based goals.

A second essential element for incorporation of the value ideal rests with *organizational morale*, or the attitude of each team member. If employees are cynical or resentful toward management, every project is going to be difficult to execute successfully. Low morale is not only a damaging flaw within the organization, it is infectious as well. It becomes a self-fulfilling prophecy once poor attitudes begin, ultimately destroying incentive. When morale is at its lowest, even positively minded project leaders will have great difficulty instilling a positive, results-oriented mindset among the team. It is not impossible, but it is difficult. At such times, creating a pocket of focused teamwork is the only way to cure the morale dilemma.

Low morale is a problem for management in the sense that the symptom often results from a distance in communication between the boardroom and the rank and file. If employees sense that executives are overpaid, ineffective, and insensitive to their needs, morale is going to suffer. One of the most effective historical attributes of Six Sigma, notably as a method for executing projects successfully, has been the improvement of organizational morale. This is accomplished by removing organizational rank from the team approach. As a revolutionary idea, this may seem extraordinary; as a means for efficiently offsetting low morale, it has been very effective. The multiyear experience at General Electric when Six Sigma was the accepted way of operations could be expressed in terms of dollar savings (and often is), if only because the bottom line is the best known method for quantifying management effectiveness. But there was more. The internal communication was vastly improved in the Six Sigma culture, and this ensured high morale. So whether you operate within Six Sigma or not, the key to overcoming low organizational morale is to instill the cultural team approach to projects.

Organizational morale also determines the level of *team spirit* within your project team (as well as within your department, operating unit, and overall organization). Team spirit can make project management an entirely satisfactory and joyful experience, because it assumes that everyone is working toward the same teamwide and organization-wide goal. The opposite is suspicion and lack of communication with conflicting goals within the team itself (for example, when the team members perceive that a project leader is using the team to advance personal career goals or to claim all of the credit for the team's efforts). Team spirit is often viewed as the defining feature of a well-led team, and new people can dispute this claim. Effective leadership—whether of a team, a department, or a platoon—requires that the entire team evolves through mutual trust and respect and that there is complete agreement in defining the immediate and long-range goals of the team. In combat, a platoon functions as a team when every member protects the others, when the short-term goal is survival, and when the long-term goal is defeating the enemy. In any organizational environment, the platoon analogy is easily expressed and well understood, although the short-range and long-range goals are normally more complex and layered within the team's function and interaction to departments and often competing organizational interests. So if a team's work is perceived as a threat to a department, the affected supervisor may resist change and operate with anything but team spirit. At this point, your task is to demonstrate how and why the project represents positive change (greater efficiency, less repetition due to lower occurrence of defects, improved value chain on many levels).

Finally, value chain is incorporated through *working together* both within the team and with outside-the-team stakeholders. The concept of working together is not the same as team spirit. Team members may have the spirit but experience difficulty working together. Invariably, the team (even when working together) will confront resistance from outside. So as project manager your task includes getting the team to work together as an integrated unit and getting outsiders to work together with your team. This dual challenge can be daunting, especially when neither the team nor the stakeholders are cooperating, or when everyone is unhappy with your proposed changes.

You get the team to work together by developing specific schedules and assigning duties to team members and subteams. Following up to ensure that everyone is aware of how their processes affect other team members is also important. Depending on the scope of the project, this may require continual reinforcement on your part. Working together does not always come naturally to people, and a team will often operate in a self-destructive mode rather than trusting other team members. This phenomenon is described by a behavioral concept known as the "tragedy of the commons." This concept, first published as an article, describes group behavior when individual interests are in play.*

Here is how it is described using a metaphor: A number of herders share a common piece of land, where they are allowed to let cows graze without restriction. Each individual has an incentive to graze as many cows as possible, but overgrazing ultimately destroys the pasture and none of the herders has access to it anymore. A sensible approach would be for the herders to work together by agreeing to a self-imposed limitation on the number of cows that will be grazed. The tragedy arises in observing that it takes only one herder to destroy the whole plan.

With this in mind, you as project manager can easily see how self-interest will quickly destroy the team and its efforts. As part of building a value chain within your project and its outcome, it is going to be essential to apply enough leadership to overcome self-interest among the "herders" on the team. The trust required for this has to come from you as project leader; human nature is going to be in play, and self-

---

*Garrett Hardin, "The Tragedy of the Commons," *Science*, Vol. 162, No. 3859 (December 13, 1968), pp. 1243–1248.

interest (saving a job, seeking a promotion, avoiding blame) is destructive to working together.

The same problem applies outside your team. A supervisor or manager who perceives your efforts as threatening to the department needs to be shown how the value chain is both beneficial and efficient. A middle-level manager or supervisor is constantly beset with inefficiency, inadequate budgets, time constraints, and other limitations. To turn a potential enemy into an ally who will gladly work together with you and your team, you need to demonstrate how your project will improve value, cut down on time and labor, and improve overall quality. Just as the herders in the illustration of the tragedy of the commons are going to act in self-interest unless enlightened with the facts, a manager or supervisor can be converted to an ally *only* by showing how your project is beneficial. As long as it is perceived as a threat, the project cannot be fully successful. This only increases the potential that any changes you institute will be reversed after your project is completed. Success is going to require allegiance among all stakeholders; success has to be measured in the long term and by the permanence of change. If you think of managers and supervisors as herders, your task is to demonstrate how they have to work together to save the commons (common interests) affecting their herd (the department).

Value: An Intangible Turned into a Tangible

How do you measure the effectiveness of the value chain your project creates? In every organization, methods for quantifying success are the key. Managers rely on budgets and remaining within them, marketing departments create and follow revenue-based goals, and military units track battle results. All of these measuring devices are used to decide whether projects succeed or fail.

The value chain may be intangible, but you can measure results by selecting the tangible changes that serve as intended targets for improved processes. So the value chain can be made into a tangible and measurable attribute of your project; this is essential not only to measure results for yourself and your team, but also to demonstrate to management how your results have worked.

Here are some guidelines for quantifying the value chain:

1. *Suggest in advance how success is to be measured.* The best time for definition is at the very start of a project. In addition to the tasks of setting a budget, preparing the preliminary completion schedule, and choosing a team, recommend methods for measuring the success of the project. Select not only the desired final outcome, but periodic accomplishments you intend to reach at phases throughout the course of the project. These interim and final goals present management with a method for determining the degree of success and provide you with specific goals.

2. *Develop tracking methods to ensure that value measurement goals are being met.* Just as a budget is tracked by variances to judge its effectiveness, a project is best judged by measuring its progress against a specific series of goals. These may consist of completion deadlines for major phases, the determination of the sources of variances or defects, and the implementation of new procedures and controls. By setting goals and then tracking progress, you are able to both quantify and define the value chain throughout the course of the project.

3. *As the project moves forward, look for additional value chain measurements.* No matter how thoroughly you define the elements of your project, it will evolve and change as you begin executing its phases. Most projects evolve in this way. Project managers face the task of adjusting schedules and budgets and, on occasion, team members—all due to the evolving nature of a project. While this is taking place, also look for additional ways that the value chain itself has to be measured. As projects change, so will the definition of value and of the value chain.

4. *Match value chain–based outcomes to expectations as a method for defining success for every project.* Also remember that, as the value chain takes on shape and definition, outcomes are going to vary as well. Be sure to match these changing criteria to the methods by which you measure success. You are going to discover that some project goals will change as you discover new value chain elements, and flexibility is crucial to ensure that the project succeeds.

5. *Don't be afraid to make changes, even to project goals.* One of the pitfalls in project management is to begin with a set of assumptions and goals that are not realistic. As your project moves forward, you are likely to discover that new and unexpected requirements arise, demanding new controls, procedures, and value chain definitions. The most logical step is to boldly document these variations and communicate them to management, recommending revised outcome expectations. Effective project management demands flexibility, not only in terms of the well-known budgets and schedules, but also of the value chain and final outcome.

Value chain management is really nothing more than ensuring that the steps you take to implement improvements are sensible, profitable, and efficient. The definition of *value* itself requires these elements as well as permanence. A project makes sense only if well-designed changes remain in effect after the project team disperses.

WORK PROJECT

1. Describe how value chain and quality are similar, as well as how they differ from one another.

2. Explain the importance of organizational morale in relation to how value is added to the project.

3. Describe why suggesting in advance how a project's success can be measured is a smart idea.

10

Writing the Supporting Documentation

If a cluttered desk is the sign of a cluttered mind,
what is the significance of a clean desk?

—LAURENCE J. PETER—

Two project team members, exhausted after a week of working against deadline, were still in the office at 7:30 P.M.

"I'm having trouble following this network diagram," the first one said. "I feel like a rat running through a maze."

"That explains it," the second one replied. "All week, I've had a craving for cheddar cheese."

How do you manage a project when you also have to train core team members as you proceed? Imagine this: You have constructed a detailed network diagram and tied down all of the loose ends for your project. Your team members know what you expect, but they are confused by the complexity of the diagram itself. In other words, rather than studying concentrated areas of responsibility and looking at the steps in each box, they are overwhelmed by the entirety of the diagram itself. This problem persists even after you get people started. Team members are not sure how they are supposed to execute their tasks.

The network diagram only identifies the sequence of execution, shows where weak links occur, and lists what each team member will do and when. But even if you pick the most qualified team members, you may need to supply more information and exercise more supervision. You cannot just list out the duties and expect them to be completed. This is especially true when:

■ *Your team includes inexperienced people.* You cannot assume that every project team is going to consist of experienced self-starters. It is more likely that even the seasoned team member is going to require some degree of supervision. If the team members' tasks are different from their departmental routines, training will also be required as a part of the process. Just as you work directly with your departmental employees, you will have to allot time to work directly with team members, helping them to understand the specific steps to a task or guiding them through an entire phase. If the supervision and training demands take time away from monitoring and other duties, you could run into a scheduling problem.

■ *The project is exceptionally complicated.* Some projects are more technical than others. Even when you do not expect to face difficulties, they may arise because you did not anticipate them. Even when core team members possess a particular array of skills, they may not know how to apply those skills in an especially complicated situation. In those circumstances, you will need to spend time working through the problems with team members.

■ *You have a very specific idea.* You want to complete your project in a specific manner to achieve the desired end result (e.g., a report) that best responds to the assignment. In such a case, you need to plan well ahead so that each team member's contribution is aimed at the result you want and isn't just executed in the most expedient way. In addition, you need to ensure that team members approach tasks using the standards you have set. For example, in studying a set of statistics from a study, you must ensure that interpretation of results is managed in an unbiased manner. That requires the application of strict standards, further requiring close supervision.

▨ *Your team consists of employees from several departments.* When you work with a team of employees from your department only, you can supervise their efforts directly. This occurs when a project is assigned within one department, which is a common occurrence. However, when your core team includes people from several different departments, or when they are from other divisions or outside the company altogether, it's not as simple. You may have to provide instructions in far greater detail when you do not have daily contact, to ensure that deadlines are met and that contributors understand their assignments.

Project Narratives

When team members need supervision and training, you can save time by preparing narrative instructions. These narratives do not need to be extensive; you certainly won't have the time to write a 100-page training manual for a three-week project. Narratives are needed only for especially complex tasks within a phase. At times, a short list of steps or results is all you need.

Instructions are helpful for core team members who otherwise would not know how to complete a task. Just as employees in your department sometimes need more than the average amount of supervision, core team members cannot be expected to always perform tasks without problems.

Example 1

One phase of your project calls for the design of a simplified form. You know your team member is familiar with this process because she has designed forms in the past. Thus, you do not need to write an extensive narrative of instructions. However, you may need to write down a list of guidelines for such information to be captured on the form. It may be very brief. For example, your instructions might be written as follows:

Design a new form, capturing the following information: name, date, description of the order, part number, brief description, number ordered, price, and total for each list; plus subtotal, tax, and final total. Please also submit your draft of the form for review and approval.

When you work from the network diagram, consider the need for narrative backup at each step. To reduce the volume of extra material and work, keep narratives as short as possible, and avoid explaining the obvious. Describe processes or provide guidelines only when steps are not self-explanatory or when you expect questions to arise. Remember, too, that no matter how carefully you develop narratives, you must still provide direct supervision and support in many instances.

Your core team members will find brief narratives helpful and reassuring as they proceed, especially when they are not accustomed to working from a network diagram. Many projects are executed haphazardly, with few controls and without the organizational support that a diagram provides. Thus, expect to run into resistance to the diagram itself. People tend to resist structure when they are not used to it, and until your team members are trained to think in terms of sequence and process, they won't be comfortable working from the diagram.

It often is necessary to describe the entire project even before your team is selected since you will not know how to compose your team until after a preliminary network diagram has been done. Don't make the mistake of picking a team first and then altering the work to fit the team—assuming you have the luxury of approaching the project more logically. It makes more sense to pick your team only after you know what skills are required. In practice, however, you may have a team imposed on you (as discussed in Chapter 3). In that case, you will have to train people to execute the tasks required for completion of the project.

The organized approach is especially helpful when your team is selected first; then the combination of network diagram and narrative instructions is an excellent training tool. For example, a project may be assigned to you and your department without authorization to recruit team members from outside. As undesirable and inflexible as this might be, it is unavoidable at times.

In such cases, narrative guidelines should be provided specifically for a task and for the person involved, not for the entire phase. Don't confuse team members by trying to cover too much material in a single narrative. Take it one step at a time, and carefully cross-reference your brief narratives to the appropriate box on the diagram.

Example 2

You are managing a project to revise procedures in a processing department. During one phase, two different team members will be working at the same time to design a new form. One will gather information to go on the form, and the other will draft the form itself. Your goal is to write brief narratives explaining how you want the job done. Your first draft reads:

> Design a new form. Arrange information in the same order found on source documents, using the information supplied by the team member gathering information. Submit your draft to the project manager for review and approval.

This instruction is likely to confuse both team members because the two tasks are described in a single paragraph. Different activities are being described at the same time. Consider breaking out the procedure into Work Breakdown Structure (WBS) outline form, which can be expressed as follows:

Design a New Form

    Team Member 1
        A. Gather information:
            Refer to source documents to identify the sequence of information. List the sequence and submit to team member 2 for form design.

Team Member 2
> B. Draft the new form:
>> Draft a new form listing information in the sequence provided above. Strive for simplicity.
> C. Obtain approval:
>> Submit the draft to the project manager for review and approval.

In the redrafted version, this project phase is presented in a logical sequence. It distinguishes the steps involved and separates out the duties by team member. Each activity is listed as a separate step and should correspond to a box on the network diagram.

More Than Paperwork

You might begin your project believing that the people on your team are capable of executing their tasks without additional training or supervision. But while they may possess the skills that brought them to your team, they often will need clarification—especially when processes are complicated. This is likely to occur when multiple tasking is going on, or when your diagram contains a loop, a point where processing could proceed in more than one direction.

Team members are likely to understand processing steps when one step follows another in a single line. However, confusion arises when one of three loops shows up on your network diagram; this is where brief narratives are helpful.

A loop requires a positive or a negative response: correct/incorrect, yes/no, or complete/incomplete, for example. Loops occur in three broad circumstances, as shown in Figure 10-1 and explained here:

1. *Verification loop.* This occurs when a team member needs to check information before proceeding. The "verify" step results in something being correct or incorrect. Work does not proceed if the verification shows something to be incorrect; it is necessary to go to the previous step and repeat the activity that was checked.

Example: At a point in your network diagram, you show a loop in

Figure 10-1. Three types of loops.

VERIFICATION LOOP

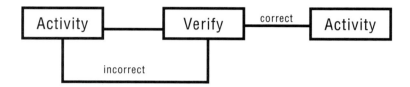

DECISION LOOP

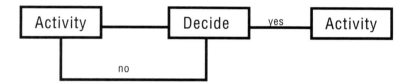

REPETITION LOOP

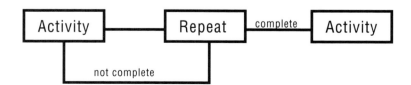

the form of a question. The box reads, "Is the balance correct?" Two lines proceed from the box. If the answer is yes (meaning the balance is correct), the process moves forward. If the answer is no (meaning the balance is incorrect), the process goes back to the previous step where the error is found and fixed. To supplement your network diagram, you write a brief narrative of the decision point. It reads:

> Is the balance correct? Check the balance on the worksheet by cross-footing. If it is correct, go to the next step. If the balance is not correct, return to the previous step; check the numbers transferred to the worksheet; and add once again to find the error.

2. *Decision loop.* The decision step is a common occurrence in projects. A yes response takes the process in one direction; a no response sends the process in another direction.

Example: At one step, the team member is asked to find historical information. The question reads, "Is the information complete?" If the answer is yes, the process moves to the next step. If the answer is no, a secondary process is required listing necessary steps to find and compile information before going forward.

In some cases, the decision loop involves possible consultation with someone else.

Example: Upon completion of a rough draft of a new form, the team member submits it to you for review and approval. If you approve the form, the process continues. If you want changes, the team member needs to revise and submit another draft. Your narrative for this situation might read:

> Submit the rough draft for approval. Present your rough draft to the project manager. If the manager approves the design, proceed to the next step. If the manager suggests changes, return to the previous step ("Design a new form") and make revisions as indicated. Then return to this step.

3. *Repetition loop.* This takes place when an activity is repeated more than once. The loop response is either "complete" or "not complete."

Example: A step calls for documenting tasks for each of three people in the department. The activity is applied to each series of tasks and is repeated three times. Thus, a repetition loop is used on the network diagram. Your narrative might read:

> Document tasks. Write brief descriptions of the tasks executed by the first person in the department. Repeat this step for the second and third persons as well. When all task descriptions have been completed, proceed to the next step. If all task descriptions have not been completed, repeat this step.

If loops confuse team members, clarify the idea by accompanying each loop instance with a narrative explanation. The narratives are not part of the network diagram, but are supplemental. Be sure to separate each set of narratives by area of responsibility to maintain a separation between duties and to keep each team member's activities as clear as possible.

Your goal should be to ensure that all core team members are able to follow their areas of responsibility on the network diagram and have the added support of narrative assistance when and where needed. This enables them to complete tasks with a minimum of supervision.

Simplifying Instructions

For some projects, you will need to develop very little in the way of narrative support. But for others, you may need to supply core team members with complete and extensive instructions. Base your decision on the mix of people on your team, the complexity of the project and its phases, and the level of concurrent activity.

Example 1

You manage a project with twelve team members. As many phases will be under way at the same time, so your network diagram is especially complicated. In this case, narrative support can help clarify each core team member's responsibility, steps, and timing. And because each activity section begins and ends with weak links (i.e., processes moving between areas of responsibility), those links can be easily planned for in advance.

Example 2

You manage a project with only a few team members, all of whom work in your department. There are only a few instances of concurrent phasing. You supply narrative support only in those areas of exceptional complexity, or where you have specific requirements that you want met.

. . . .

The purpose of narratives is to provide more detail than team members have with the network diagram. The diagram places each step and phase in perspective and shows the team members the overall scope (as well as their specific contribution). This is valuable when team members work in relative isolation from the overall project processes. The network diagram provides team members with perspective and gives the project a visual character. Very seldom will a group of people sit in a room and work together. It's more likely that teamwork proceeds when people or groups break off and execute phases on their own—coordinated as part of the whole but working alone.

The reality of teamwork such as this challenges your leadership abilities. You need to ensure that your team members share their collective duties and work well together; you must also explain how each member's part fits in the big picture. The network diagram illustrates this in the best possible way—by showing the critical path process while breaking out individual areas of responsibility. Wise leaders know that the best way to lead is to help team members feel included in the larger scheme of things.

To tie the network diagram to step-by-step narratives for the more complex portions of work, it helps to reproduce segments of the network diagram next to narrative descriptions. This approach gives you and your team several benefits:

■ *It makes the flowchart easier to read.* We retain information gathered visually more readily than information obtained from narratives alone. The network diagram is visual because it imposes a pattern on the project and its phases. If narratives are separate, your team has to connect one representation of the process to the other. By reproducing the visual and narrative in the same place, retention is improved vastly.

■ *It identifies each step directly.* Team members may be intimidated by the scope and complexity of their tasks when reviewed in diagram form alone. But when they are broken down and addressed directly as single steps in the process, team members can develop greater confidence in their ability to respond.

■ *It reverts to vertical steps.* People are accustomed to thinking of processes in top-to-bottom form. This is why vertical flowcharts are comfortable and familiar to most people. As inefficient as the vertical flowchart is, people may comprehend their steps more easily when the horizontal version is elaborated upon by combining it with a vertical workflow and narrative.

The Diagram/Narrative Combination

The complex network diagram can be converted into a fairly simple series of steps, divided into specific areas of responsibility. This improves the team's comprehension and summarizes individual tasks and roles. The problem is that extensive summaries take time to create, so they should be used only for the more complex segments of the process.

Example 1

One phase in your project is entitled "Prepare worksheet." This phase includes a verification loop. The steps are depicted in Figure 10-2.

Anticipating that some team members may find the steps to follow confusing, you write narrative explanations of the process. To help in tracking the steps, you reproduce the boxes from the diagram next to

Figure 10-2. Verification loop.

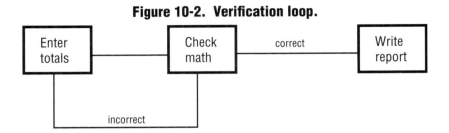

the narrative descriptions. An example of this technique is shown in Figure 10-3.

Notice how the horizontal steps on the network diagram are duplicated vertically in the narrative section. People are comfortable with top-to-bottom flowcharts because that is how they read; this technique conforms to the familiar learning pattern while preserving the advantages of the flowchart. By breaking out a small portion of the network diagram and isolating it along with narrative support, you help team members to overcome confusion and to more effectively master the use of process flowcharts.

Treatment of the loop is also easy to follow. In the diagram, the loop is probably the most confusing part, because the process splits and team members have to decide how and why and what they need to do at that point. The narrative/diagram combination explains and clarifies the process for the team member.

The narrative/diagram combination is also useful for elaborating upon weak links and bringing them to team members' attention. Because narratives are prepared for each team member individually, they tend to begin and end with weak links. So one area of responsibility takes up where another finishes.

In the previous example, the team members start to prepare the worksheet upon receipt of a report from the accounting department. And when the worksheet has been prepared and a subsequent report written, that work is passed on to the project manager. The beginning and end points of this process are weak links.

The narrative supplement helps every member of your core team to manage these weak links because:

Figure 10-3. Narrative/flowchart combination.

Refer to the report submitted by the accounting department. It lists the totals of estimated transactions processed by the five processing departments in our division.

Enter the totals from the accounting department report on the worksheet you are preparing. The information you enter should correspond with the column heading you wrote in previously.

When you have completed that step, check the math for each column and for each row. Make certian the worksheet is in balance.

If the worksheet is not in balance, return to the previous step. Check each number against the accounting report. Locate all errors and correct the worksheet. Check math once again.

When the worksheet is in balance, proceed to the next step.

Write a report summarizing the information entered on the worksheet. Submit the report to the project manager for review. Include the worksheet with the report so that the manager will be able to verify the information.

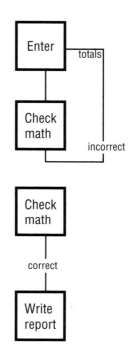

- The process itself cannot begin until the previous steps have been completed and passed on.

- The process is not complete until the last step, which often involves passing results to the next person or area of responsibility.

As project manager, you will find that the easiest way to control the schedule is by tracking the timeline on the network diagram. The visual summary is helpful as well, because it helps you track progress for the entire project, no matter how many concurrent phases are under way at the same time. Many scheduling problems come as a surprise when it's too late to help team members work through them; the network diagram helps you to prevent that.

Project Control Documentation

Because every project is different, no exact level of documentation is going to be appropriate in every case. It has to be dictated by need. In some cases, you will need a very formal, elaborate series of documents that show not only the progress of activity, but also define areas of responsibility. This can help to avoid overlaps in execution, especially when your project team is spread out over several different departments and includes a large number of people.

In that case, overall documentation will be similar to engineering specifications. Several levels of definition are required for the larger project: responsibility for each phase, scope of their responsibilities, materials they will need, appearance of the end result, and interim deadline. This requirement is made more complex when team members act as floaters among several different areas of responsibility. These areas are not always fixed and permanent but may evolve from one phase to another. This complicates not only the team's actions, but your role in coordinating the whole project.

With exceptionally large project teams, phases have to be broken down according to their complexity. In some cases, you need to assign primary responsibility to one team member as well as secondary roles for others. The schedule may require considerable detail in these circumstances, and additional support may be helpful in the form of a detailed WBS outline, Gantt chart, and Critical Path Method (CPM) diagram. These additional tools should be coordinated with a more summarized version of sequence and deadline, expressed on the network diagram.

The especially complex project—one taking up many months and demanding a large project team—is better defined and controlled with narrative support that's helpful enough so that all team members know what is expected and how they should proceed.

Example

Your project requires the development of procedures for a department currently processing information manually. This department has been passed over for automation because it deals with many exceptions. Other than document production, which is automated, the processes in this department involve special problems and exceptions. However, the time has come to automate, given increased volume and work activity. The company wants the department automated within six months, and your project will achieve several end results:

- Definition of required input formats and expected monthly transaction volume

- Procedures for input, verification, and documentation

- Design of input and control forms

- Design of database elements

- Design of reports drawn from the database for an array of reporting and follow-up requirements

- Procedures for retraining of employees

Team members for this project will include several people from the subject department, members of your department, and a systems analyst. You will also work with outside consultants. You will need to develop narrative support on several levels, including:

- Instructions for your project team relating to the gathering of information about current procedures and system requirements

▓ Methods to be employed in drafting initial results and submitting them for approval

▓ Guidelines for writing new procedures, designing forms, and communicating with the systems analyst and technical staff

Because this project involves team members working in other departments (and outside the company), it is critical to define areas of responsibility with great care before getting into the process. You define areas of responsibility in three ways, according to:

1. *Type of work*. An employee in your department will be responsible for drafting the database files for the new system, working closely with the systems analyst and the outside consultant. Another employee from your department is given a series of tasks relating to the design of forms.

2. *Individuals who possess special knowledge or skills*. The systems analyst plays a pivotal role in this project because development of new, automated procedures are involved. Employees in the subject department, by virtue of their jobs, know what has to be accomplished and can assist in defining how automation can continue to meet the department's needs.

3. *Phases of the project*. A phase, by its nature, dictates which individuals on your team should be given a specific responsibility. When the team is large, you must delegate, choosing team members to act in primary roles and supervising the work of others.

· · · · · · · · · · ·

The documentation you create, whether very limited and brief, or detailed and extensive, helps you monitor your project and remain on schedule. Hopefully, it will also assist in defining areas of responsibility well enough so that each core team member knows exactly what you expect, when and how it needs to be completed, and how to proceed with minimal supervision.

With the proper documentation—notably a combination of a network diagram and narratives where required—you have the tools to successfully lead your project team toward timely completion of its work. To ensure this, you also need to develop systems for periodic review, including progress reporting, deadline control, budget reporting and variance corrections, and actions designed to make up early delays later on. Project review is the topic of the next chapter.

WORK PROJECT

1. You are writing narrative instructions for a project phase involving two team members and a decision step. The sequence of activities is as follows:

- Team member 1 prepares an outline of tasks and gives the outline to team member 2.
- Team member 2 reviews the outline. If he has any questions, he meets with team member 1 and asks for more information.
- Once team member 2 has the information needed, he prepares a step-by-step flowchart of the procedures.

How would you combine narratives with activity and decision boxes to describe these steps for each of the two team members?

2. Describe the typical features of:
   a. Verification loops
   b. Decision loops
   c. Repetition loops

3. Describe and explain three ways that areas of responsibility are defined in a project narrative document.

11

Conducting the Project Review

*For all the intellect and technique a manager can muster,
his success turns on a subtle and elusive quality—the
degree to which he can stimulate people to make the most
of their own inherent capabilities.*

—LESTER R. BITTEL—

"I think there's too much bureaucracy in this company," one manager confided to another. "Last month, the president formed a task force to figure out why projects weren't being finished on schedule."

"I know. It struck me as a good idea," the other manager replied.

"Except for one thing. They haven't submitted their report yet, and it was due three weeks ago."

One very successful project manager explained how she never went over budget or missed a deadline: constant review and monitoring. Never satisfied with the plan as originally conceived, she spent at least as much time following the team's progress as she spent involved in the work itself.

Your role, of course, is to keep your team working toward the final deadline, within the budget, and in line with the goals of the project—and on a broader field, to produce a result of the highest possible quality and accuracy. This effort may take more time than actual participation in the work of the project; and perhaps it should.

Defining Success

The importance of leading your team, staying within the budget, and meeting schedule deadlines may prevent you from the broader question: How do you know whether your project is a success? In all organizational efforts, but especially in projects, defining success goes beyond the schedule and budget, even when these issues dominate the interests of management and even of project managers and team members.

Remember these attributes to define success for your own projects:

1. *Expectations have been met on all levels.* Although often overlooked, everyone with an interest in the project has a set of expectations. For this reason, it makes sense to start out the project by making a list of stakeholders' expectations and then build these into the desired results. No matter how effectively you lead your team, meet your deadlines, and come in under budget, the project succeeds only if the stakeholders are pleased with the final results.

2. *Everyone wins based on the final outcome.* Stakeholder expectations form a foundation for defining success, but it is also important for all of your team members to have a sense of accomplishment and for management to appreciate the outcome. This means not only that all involved are happy with the effort, but also that no one is deprived along the way. A project creating benefit for one group at the expense of another is only going to add to the political tension and rivalry within the organization. Looking for the win/win outcome always works out better.

3. *Quality has been created as part of the new procedure.* The Six Sigma approach requires that quality dominates all processes and that all projects are focused on this ideal. Whether you use a formalized Six Sigma program or not, quality has to be maintained or improved. A project that streamlines time and costs but also reduces quality is not successful, because the lower quality is ultimately going to more than offset any apparent savings.

4. *New value was created through risk management and controls.* The most successful projects create new value without adding new expense. For example, simple changes in processing may reduce defects without adding to costs or time; they may even reduce the cost elements of processes. This usually requires the installation of risk management as part of the process, through improved controls within the process itself, not as an outside auditing or oversight function.

5. *The goals of the project have been met.* Finally, the big question comes down to whether your efforts have reached management's original goals. If a goal of your project was to reduce expenses, cut processing time, improve customer responses, or eliminate repetitive defects, your question has to be whether the project accomplished those goals. It is interesting that, as some projects evolve, you may begin with one set of goal assumptions only to discover a more expanded set of problems that need to be addressed. So project management often is a dynamic process that requires continual communication with management, redefinition, and perhaps revision of schedules and budgets. A periodic progress review is essential for this reason; you may need to ensure that your project is moving along scheduling and budgetary expectations; you may also need to change the goals of the original project.

The Progress Review

It may appear that a "successful" project is one that is completed on time and within budget. In fact, though, these obvious objectives can be controlled and are more likely to come about when your team members have a sense of their own participation. It helps greatly if team members have a sense of ownership in the project and not merely a reporting role. Problems leading to schedule and budget failure are not always merely chance events, but reflect other problems your team has to face. These problems can include inadequate supervision or training, low morale (coming from a sense of not having a real stake in the outcome), or inadequate time to devote to the project (often due to departmental demands or lack of support from a team member's supervisor). It is never a pleasant experience to be involved in a project that has been given inadequate time, a minimal budget, and no support from above.

Certainly, anyone in a managerial role is all too familiar with what can go wrong in a project, not to mention in a department, division, or even companywide. As project manager, you can effectively overcome the internal problems that are inherent in all efforts, assuming that you are not facing an impossible deadline with an overworked staff and no budget! That may be a rather larger assumption; however, even with those handicaps, you can take steps to review progress and control the project's budgeting and scheduling issues in three primary ways:

1. *Define standards of performance.* What do you expect from your team? The obvious answer—meeting phase and project deadlines within budget—are always primary objectives. Beyond these questions, however, are the equally critical objectives of quality, cooperation, and results. Thus, your project review needs to consist of checking for accuracy and thoroughness (e.g., correct interpretation of raw data), achievement of team ideals (e.g., removal of bias in applying results), and comprehensive results (e.g., double-checking all numerical reports).

2. *Find appropriate applications of the standards.* As your project moves forward, how do you test the standards you have set, and what do your tests reveal? This is where project review is most likely to be lacking. It is not enough to remain on schedule and within budget. You may work well with your core team in defining standards at the beginning of the project; you also need to monitor the progress of the project with those standards in mind.

3. *Decide what actions, if any, you need to take.* What should you do upon discovering problems? Your team may be falling behind schedule, for example. That is a problem in itself, but it often is a symptom of a broader team problem as well. Getting back on schedule often is not as difficult as solving the underlying problem. It could be related to teamwork, ability, communication, effort, authority, or motivation. Identifying what is really going on and then taking action to solve it are two areas where your leadership insight will be keenly tested.

Difficult-to-Define Problem Areas

Understanding what is going on at the team level—in the trenches, so to speak—may seem easy and obvious. But one aspect of being a leader is that you lose touch, at least to a degree, with the realities the team members face. The most severe of problems are sometimes kept from the manager for a variety of reasons, and these often are the least visible and most difficult issues to solve. You will discover, however, that by making a sincere effort to make your team's work easy and successful, you will have a significant and positive effect on team morale. Improvement in morale (or attitude) often solves all of the other problems on your project.

Another question faced by every project manager is that of quality control. How do you determine whether your team is adhering to the standards you have set? Is your team working as a team, or as a group of individuals forced together in the name of the project? Are some people doing more than their share and others less? These are the questions you need to ask continuously, because only by inquiring in these areas can you prevent the kinds of less tangible problems from occurring that often prevent the team from complying with the more obvious goals of finishing the project on time and within budget. It's in those intangible and difficult-to-define areas that your leadership is tested and proved.

Your standards vary from one project to another, naturally. For example, a project involving research (e.g., compiling, interpreting, and reporting information) demands a particular adherence to accuracy, removal of bias, and attention to detail. The same high level of team operational standards will not apply to every other project. If your work results in a report to be presented to management, you need to ensure that all of the details have been checked. This means the report should be professional in every aspect. Information should be arranged logically, cross-referenced where necessary, and indexed if required by the volume of information. It should also be checked for spelling and grammar as well as mathematical accuracy. These small details define the professionalism of the report and will determine whether the reader places confidence in the report.

These small but important details define "excellence" as you apply it to your project. The way that you apply these standards reflects not only your team's work overall, but your leadership abilities as well.

Period versus Ongoing Review

How frequently should you review your team's progress? Some managers approach review in a formal manner; others see review as an ongoing part of their function as project manager. However you approach the review process, keep the important questions in mind, relating not only to budget and schedule, but also to the less tangible questions about quality control, standards, and team morale.

The ongoing approach makes more sense than the periodic review. Remember, the project does not run like a department. Virtually all of the functions of the project are exceptional, whereas departments run on routine. Problems tend to arise in projects suddenly and unexpectedly, become irreversible too quickly, and can have a significant impact on the entire flow of work. The best project manager is always striving to remain one step ahead of such problems, solving them before they get out of hand. Waiting until a problem comes to your attention often means it is too late. Take a preventive approach, looking for the emerging problem and attacking it in order to protect your team from disruption and delay.

Project Leadership Attributes

As project manager, you are continually expected to prevent problems by anticipating them and taking the right steps before the relatively simple problem turns into a crisis. Project leadership varies considerably from department supervision or management, in several ways:

1. ***The team is a focus in the project; the routine is the focus in the department.*** The project is a unique structure due to the nonrecurring nature of its work. Because of this, it is a mistake for a manager experienced in supervising or managing a department to proceed on the assumption that a project team is merely a form of specialized departmentlike unit. In fact, the team is quite different because it is expected to perform specialized, nonrecurring work. As project manager, your focus has to be on working closely with, training, mentoring, and helping the team; the routine itself is secondary to this.

2. ***Project goals are specific to the project and are finite; the department's goals are more generalized and permanent.*** The project goals you and your team need to accomplish are nonrecurring and quite specific. A department may not even operate on specific goals because it has a generalized purpose, a series of recurring tasks and routines, and a permanent requirement for repetitive cyclical task completion.

3. ***Project leadership involves skillful oversight of people who do not work together; departmental leadership is more like an organizational family.*** Even the most experienced supervisor should expect to encounter some problems getting project teams to work together harmoniously. People within a department tend to work together as a sort of family unit, with varying levels of power and influence at play. The project team is a new and different structure. Just as strangers sharing a house are going to have to work out their rules for getting along with each other, team members are all new to the scene. The project team is not the same as the familylike department.

4. ***Managers of projects often have to be more involved with team members because tasks are not repetitive; in a department, employees often generate their work and complete tasks as a matter of routine.*** As project manager, you may need to also train and teach team members. Supervisors in departments rely on rou-

tine and repetition to handle most issues, and the exceptions that arise require them to step in and help. A project is *all* management by exception; none of the tasks you expect team members to perform are repetitive, and some team members are not going to know how to innovate in an unfamiliar environment.

5. *Project managers have to rely on team members for their own weak areas; supervisors are expected to have all of the skills.* Project managers are expected to possess organizational and leadership skills, even when they do not have all the experience required for each phase of a project. Thus, you have to rely on team members to supply specialized expertise. In comparison, the supervisor of a department is expected to be familiar with every possible situation that is going to arise within the departmental routines. Supervisors are experts in a limited venue, and project managers are generalists with management skills.

6. *Schedules and budgets are short term in projects, but cycle driven in departments.* Some project managers make the mistake of tying budgets and schedules to the familiar cyclical deadline they use in a department. A project, however, has its own cycles, and these are never the same as the business or accounting cycle, in which a budget and sales month end on the last day of the month. So the control aspects of your project have to be freed from the normal cyclical norms of the organization, and operated on an entirely unique schedule, dictated by the requirements of the project, not by a monthly closing date.

Monitoring and Reporting

You need to report progress on two levels. First, you communicate with the team, which is an opportunity to acknowledge effort, motivate individuals, and demonstrate your desire for team participation. It also serves as a chance to identify emerging problems, propose solutions, and make adjustments in the schedule for conflicts. Second, you report to management, either to the person who gave you the project assignment or to a group of executives.

Reporting to the Team

Your report to the team is a form of performance review. Since you expect core team members to work together under your leadership, it also makes sense to report to the entire group. This can take place during periodic team meetings. These should be brief and action-oriented.

Schedule team meetings at critical junctures in the schedule. For example, at a point where a particularly complex phase is about to begin, a team meeting can address problems you anticipate. Large, especially complicated projects lend themselves to several report/review meetings; smaller, less complex projects require only one or two set meetings and additional ones if needed. If you are working with a large team and there is concurrent phasing, meetings may have to be included in the schedule as part of the phase itself.

Reporting to Management

Your report to management is likely to be more formal but less detailed than the team meetings. Here, your concern is not with the minutiae of execution and interim problems, but more with the broad overview. Bigger questions of overall schedule and budget and any problems connected to those concerns should be a part of the progress report.

Even though you may not be required to present a progress report, you may consider suggesting such a policy, especially for longer-term, larger-budget projects. Budget and schedule review are essential in larger projects. Whether you are required to make such a report or you suggest it yourself, be sure you are prepared. Present your status report in writing, even if you are also giving a verbal summary. For larger projects, also ask for brief reports from team subgroup leaders, and include these with your report.

What should your status report contain, and how long should it be? The report to management should contain only the information required to convey the information necessary. Avoid putting in details that really aren't of concern to management. Limit your report to four broader topics:

1. Describe the project and its deadline briefly.

2. Describe the current status of schedule and budget.

3. Explain any variances and their causes, or schedule delays.

4. Summarize your expectations for the future (i.e., the completion and deadline).

The discussion of schedule and budget can be summarized on a single page of your report. It helps to include a Gantt chart that provides a nice overview of the project. Don't include the network diagram, which is far too much detail and unnecessary for reporting to management.

If your project is on schedule and within budget, the entire report can be very brief. When further explanation is required, try to identify specific problems in terms of possible solutions. Demonstrate that whatever problems you are facing, you are trying to overcome those problems, rather than delegating upward by merely presenting the problem in your report.

Example

You are presenting a report on the status of your project. You are on schedule, but you expect to run into problems in the coming month. The accounting department was supposed to provide information to you, but the manager of that department recently told you that it was going to be late. She had been given an unexpected job and its deadline is a priority. She simply doesn't have the staff to complete the work promised to you, and it will delay your project two weeks.

An important point to remember concerning your report to management is this: Missing a promised deadline is not always a disaster. In fact, in some cases, management accepts delays as normal. To a degree, a deadline is a standard against which to measure progress; it isn't necessarily a hard-and-fast requirement. As project manager, however, you should always know whether the deadline is intended to be only a guideline or whether it is a mandate. It is a disaster, in any case, to fail to inform management that a deadline cannot be met. Your report should be as accurate as possible and should not leave out any important information—even when it is bad news.

In the previous example, there are two ways to disclose the problem. One is to place blame, which does not solve the problem; in fact, it makes matters worse because it puts management in the position of having to decide what to do about it. Another method is to offer constructive solutions. For example, your report might read, "The project will be delayed two weeks; a scheduling conflict will prevent the production of essential information from the accounting department." It may also state, "Based on the current schedule, the project will be two weeks late in completion. A possible solution is to provide additional staffing to assist the accounting department so that the project can remain on schedule."

In this last case, you propose a solution to the problem without placing blame. Chances are, the other manager can do nothing to solve your schedule delay, and who is to blame is not a constructive topic for your report. Proposed solutions are far more revealing about the character of the project—and of the project manager.

If you make recommendations that would affect another department, it is also wise to first consult with the manager and mention that you want to proceed with that idea. This gives the manager the chance to offer other alternatives or to advise why the recommendation could cause problems. Maintain good communication to avoid introducing new problems in the future.

The Missed Deadline

You might speculate on the question of deadlines and conclude that management is not overly concerned with timely completion. This is the unfortunate state of affairs in many companies. Deadlines are missed so regularly that it has become the norm; it is a surprise when a project is completed on time.

Set a standard. Take every deadline seriously as a promise to deliver, and consider delays as unacceptable unless they also are unavoidable. If unavoidable, management should be informed as soon as possible that the deadline cannot be met.

Remember these important points about deadlines:

■ *The deadline may have been set early on purpose.* If managers are used to missed deadlines, it could become a matter of practice to set them early—in the hope that projects will be completed by the time they really need them. For example, the president needs your report by May 1. You are given a deadline of April 1 so that the extra month provides time to meet the "real" deadline.

Setting early deadlines only encourages continuing failure to meet them. Thus, the problem is intensified rather than solved and a culture of not keeping promises goes into effect. The same problem is seen in budgets; allowances are set at one level, but management has a higher level in mind, accepting the supposedly inevitable fact that departments always exceed their budgets. This attitude, whether relating to deadlines or to budgets, only makes matters worse and subverts the intended purpose of managerial controls. Ask for a realistic deadline and then get the reputation as a project manager who meets that deadline.

■ *Management may accept missed deadlines.* Top management may not be happy about the fact that deadlines are missed more often than not, but it lives with the situation because it has become the norm. This is a symptom of a greater problem and should never be used as an excuse to miss a deadline. Management should impose realistic deadlines and then expect them to be met. Project managers should agree to that policy and strive to enforce it.

■ *Management may depend on timely delivery to decide other important matters.* To a project manager deeply involved in the details of keeping a project on schedule, the immediate phase deadline may seem like the highest priority. Remember, though, that management may be waiting for the results of your project to decide other matters. If you miss your final deadline, the consequences will be more far-reaching than your project.

■ *One of your responsibilities is to keep management up to date.* As a project manager, you are charged with the duty of advising management. Just as you are responsible for departmental schedules, budgets, and reports, you are responsible for the same matters as project manager. Missed deadlines and emerging problems (along with proposed solutions) should be communicated up the chain. The lines of communication between you and management should be characterized by constant dialogue; hopefully, information will flow in both directions.

■ *Delays may be acceptable not because they occur frequently, but because of other delays beyond your project.* Management may express little concern when you advise that your project will be delayed. Don't assume that this means your missed deadline is not a problem. It could be that other delays outside of your knowledge have made your original deadline less critical. Delay is chronic, so chances are that management is far behind schedule and your project fits into the scheme of things even with its missed deadline.

■ *You can ask for an extension.* Some project managers hesitate to advise management about delays, so they take the worst possible course: saying nothing. When you are under pressure to complete your project, you can ask for an extension if you run into unexpected problems. This is preferable to not communicating the problem at all.

■ *You might overcome delays by looking for shortcuts.* Upon review, you may be able to cut time from upcoming phases by taking shortcuts. Running phases concurrently, getting partial phases completed early, adding staff, and cutting work levels are examples of ways to reduce time. If you have built in a time cushion for later phases, that also helps. However, be sure that you do not cut into the quality or accuracy of your outcome just to meet the deadline. It's better to deliver the goods later than expected than to compromise your standards.

The Accelerated Schedule

Here is a problem you'll encounter time and again: Your project is going along efficiently and on schedule with no signs of delay. Then a single unexpected problem (e.g., discovering that a phase involves more complexity and time than anticipated) throws your whole schedule into disarray.

Being able to anticipate problems of this nature requires experience. The more time you spend managing projects, the more you'll be able to anticipate unexpected delays. You will know how to recognize the symptoms in advance. For example, if two or more weak links occur at the same schedule point, chances are higher than average that a delay will occur. Or if you are waiting for crucial information from a department or outside resource, you do not have control over the timing of delivery.

Even the most experienced project manager will encounter scheduling problems; that is unavoidable. However, skill comes into play in the way that you respond to delays. Fast action helps make up for lost time. Not only is every project different, but every instance of delay and every cause will be different as well.

You cannot always depend on acceleration of the schedule as a solution to delays. Even when you build in slack time in later phases, delays can quickly outrun a two- to three-day allowance so that you are likely to have little flexibility toward the end. However, by improving efficiency and teamwork, you can still make up for lost time.

In addition to the common delays associated with outside resources, you may also have to overcome internal political problems. A department manager may resist cooperating with you for a variety of reasons, react in a negative way to you and your project, or refuse to provide resources or information in a timely manner, citing departmental priorities. Solutions to these problems are elusive. You can try a direct meeting, or you can ask management to intervene. Between these two choices, it is not a question of which approach is best; rather, you have to decide which is worse. Internal political problems persist because at least one side doesn't want the problem solved. So whether or not you accelerate your project, you cannot quickly overcome resistance justified by internal conflict. All you can do is try and work around the roadblock, seeking ways to finish the project without help from the other manager.

The Changing Objective

Although delays are difficult enough to deal with, they often can be anticipated. However, one of the most frustrating experiences a project manager can suffer is having the project's very definition changed while it is under way. It seems illogical that management would alter an assignment after you invest your team's efforts for many weeks (or even months) of endeavor. Realistically, though, the project's objective and definition can change for several reasons.

The ever-changing climate in your company can cause a particular project to become obsolete very rapidly, owing to economic, competitive, and capital reasons, for example. A change in management will be accompanied by a change in priorities. If turnover among executives is common in your company, your project's priority—even its existence—could be subject to turnover as well.

Even without the consequences of personnel changes, management may waver in its course. While this is disruptive and has a negative effect on team morale, it is also beyond your control. In companies led by people who lack a strong sense of purpose, indecision can become a characteristic of the entire corporate culture. Managers of departments and projects, and their subordinates, suffer directly under indecisive leadership. However, in that environment, the reality is that your original project objective may be replaced, perhaps more than once.

There is little purpose in arguing to retain the original objective once management has decided it is no longer valid. Resisting change, even illogical and disruptive change, only marks you as a troublemaker and does little for the reputation you want to encourage—namely, that you are a member of the "team" as management defines it. The fact that its definition changes frequently makes this one of the more difficult working situations; however, you need to go along until the current chaotic leadership is replaced with a more reasoned approach.

Appropriate responses to changed project definitions and objectives should include taking the following important steps:

1. ***Immediately inform your team.*** Avoid adopting an antimanagement attitude when your project's objective is changed. Explain why

the change is being made to the best of your ability. Remember that even when you disagree with management or its approach, you should never convey that feeling to subordinates. As a member of the chain of command, you are responsible for representing management's interests to your team. Keep them informed of the facts, but avoid expressing your personal feelings about the change.

2. *Concentrate on executing the change.* Avoid letting a negative attitude affect your work or your team's. Channel your energy into adjusting your efforts with the new project goal in mind. Even when your morale is low, you have a responsibility to present a role model of leadership to your team. That means maintaining a professional approach even when management has thrown your work into chaos and you have to go over the same ground again.

3. *Revise your schedule and budget.* If you need to make substantial changes (e.g., delay the project's deadline), write a brief report and submit it to management. If the change will make it necessary to change the schedule, it would be unreasonable to expect you to meet the original deadline. Keep the report positive and explain the reasons that more time will be needed.

4. *Revise your control forms.* Remember to change your Gantt chart, Critical Path Method (CPM), and network diagram to reflect the change in project objective. Essentially, a change makes the original project obsolete and replaces it with another one. Substantial change has to be carried through to all of your control systems.

You can avoid the majority of changed objectives by working to obtain a clear definition at the very beginning of the project. Most changes in objective result not from outside influences beyond your control but from lack of definition. This problem is found at all levels in the company. However, to ensure your project's success, you need to insist on a clear definition of what your project is intended to achieve. If management is unable or unwilling to be that precise, offer an objective (in writing) and ask for clarification. It is management's job to provide you with clear definition, but that doesn't mean you will receive it automatically.

When an executive avoids being pinned down to precise objectives, the greater the chances that the course of your work will be changed during the project or, even worse, the result will not be what the executive wanted. It is crucial to get a clear definition at the beginning in order to avoid wasting time on the project itself.

Staying on Course

Successful project review can be accomplished only when the project's objective remains unchanged. Once you are given a revised definition, your judgment has to be revised as well. When you begin your project, you have to assume that it will be continued through to the end as defined. That means you need guidelines and team standards, as well as a course for review. Here are five guidelines to follow:

1. *Make sure everyone on your team has a specific range of duties (i.e., an area of responsibility) and that relationships between team members are defined clearly.* With a concise and complete definition of duties for all team members or subgroups, your team will be better equipped to work together and avoid the conflicts and confusion that are seen in ill-defined projects.

2. *Do not restrict your tests of successful progress only to questions of schedules and budgets.* You also need to look for signs of team conflict or confusion and be prepared to mediate, train, and support your team as needed. The intangible problems a team faces during the course of the project can cause more severe problems than a budget variance or missed deadline. The very quality of result, not to mention overall team satisfaction, will be affected by how well the team works together and understands its assignment.

3. *Test what you can control.* Problems created by outsiders cannot be solved by any actions you might take. You can only anticipate such problems and do your best to work around them. Testing is useful only to the extent that it allows you to manage the project and to prevent problems from arising.

4. *Tackle the project with an action orientation.* Take steps to solve short-term problems while keeping one eye on the final deadline. Encourage core team members to communicate with you regularly and advise you of upcoming problems.

5. *Support your team in every important way.* Review core team members' work, but also remember that the project's success depends on your being available when team members need help. Your availability to train and instruct, and to back up team members in every way, are leadership attributes that are essential in every project.

* * * * * * * * * * *

The success of your project—and, to a greater extent, your team's sense of success—depends on how well you communicate and the tone you set for the team effort. In addition to the functions of monitoring and reviewing, you must provide for your team members' needs by offering strong leadership and direction and maintaining team and individual morale. The next chapter tackles the all-important subject of communication in the project environment.

WORK PROJECT

1. Describe the three problems you face in progress review, and explain how solving each one improves the review process.

2. Explain why it is important to review your team's progress continually. Compare project and department reviews.

3. Describe the four elements you should include in a review report to management for ongoing projects.

12

The Communication Challenge

When two men communicate with each other by word of mouth, there is a twofold hazard in that communication.

—SAM ERVIN—

A manager received a written memo. It read in part: "We must keep the lines of communication open between our departments in order to ensure the success of this project. Please call me as soon as possible so that we can discuss schedules and deadlines."

The manager told his assistant, "I'd like to answer, but whoever wrote this memo forgot to include his name."

We have all heard the clichés about communication. But putting the ideas into practice often is much harder than applying the theories. This is more true for project management than in the department.

When you manage a department, you are in constant contact with your staff. Their tasks are well defined and recurring. Your subordinates are focused on performance, and their evaluation depends on how well they execute a narrowly defined range of tasks. A project, by comparison, may be viewed as an intrusion into a well-ordered departmental rhythm, a departure from what is considered "normal"—even when the ideal of normality is difficult to achieve for any length of time.

In addition to the manager-team dynamics, you must also contend with communication on three additional levels:

1. *The Assignment.* The executive (or committee) that first assigned the project to you may not agree with your idea of what the project should achieve; the same person may have a change of mind about the outcome, sometimes without letting you know.

2. *Other Departments.* The managers of other departments have their own priorities and can be expected to have problems with your schedule, especially if it affects their workload and timing. Two situations are of special concern to you: when members of other departments are on your team, and when you need to receive information from another department.

3. *Outside Resources.* Your project could depend on help or information from outside resources—companies, consultants, suppliers, or agencies that are not part of your organization or division.

Your budget and schedule are your best communications tools. They are effective in conveying what you need to your core team members, other departments, outside resources, and management. Budgets and schedules can be used to communicate in different ways.

Communication Skills Project Managers Need

The word "communication" is often used without a true understanding of its meaning. The basic ability to express yourself in e-mail, letters, documentation, verbal discussions, and meetings describes what is usually called "communication." Some people are better at it than others, and those who do not communicate as well as they would like need to work harder to ensure that they express themselves clearly and specifically.

The lack of effective communications invariably leads to misunderstandings. A team member who does not complete a task as you ask or runs over budget may explain that you as project manager did not make yourself clear enough. Management may also blame a project manager for the same shortcomings because, upon discovery of problems, management was not informed in a timely manner.

These communications issues are usually well understood by managers and supervisors and handled as part of the normal routine or organizational life, sometimes effectively and sometimes less so. As project manager, you are going to be held to a higher standard, however. A supervisor who does not communicate well is often compensated for by employees, who know they have to ask for clarification, anticipate a supervisor's lack of ability, or work around this problem in other ways. You cannot expect the same consideration from project team members. Your communication skills have to be expanded to include four additional skill areas:

1. *You need to master the basics of project management.* Remember, managing a project is not the same as managing a department. The project team is not a temporary department, but a collection of people who do not work together all the time and who are going to require extensive knowledge from you. This demands that you become familiar with the organizational principles of project management. This is gained not only from on-the-job experience, but also from reading and from internal or external training courses. (The Project Management Institute offers courses specializing in project management skills: go to www.pmi.org and click on the link "Get Certified.")

2. *You are expected to have the technical expertise required for the job.* Every project involves a specialized area and processes, and as a basic assumption you were picked for the role of project manager because you possess the technical skills to know what needs to be changed or fixed. However, if you were given the assignment merely because you managed a different project successfully, you may need to add members to your team to provide you with this technical knowledge.

3. *Your basic management skills have to be excellent.* Project managers are in some ways expected to be supermanagers, bringing to the job not only leadership abilities, technical skills, and organizational

knowledge, but also the ability to adjust to the unexpected, overcome team conflicts, and anticipate and prevent risks. This all requires very sharp basic management skills, including abilities in budgeting, team management, training, and talent in mastering new and unexpected tasks as the project moves through its phases.

   4. *Project managers are expected to exemplify the basics of good leadership.* Finally, the intangible ability to lead effectively is all-important to project managers. Natural leaders make it look easy, but strong leadership rarely comes to anyone naturally. It requires an expanded knowledge area, experience, and the respect of team members, stakeholders, management, and anyone else you need to work with while performing your project management role.

The Budget as a Communication Tool

The budget defines a financial commitment and is intended to set a standard for measuring expenditures. If variances occur, they often are accompanied by a scheduling problem.

   Your project budget also measures degrees of risk involved with your project. All change involves risk, and when time and money are being committed and spent, the decision to proceed is made with an awareness of risk. Management will proceed with a project if it believes that the risk is justified by the outcome or necessary in the course of operations. So, for example, if you propose a project, you can communicate the idea in terms of risk and potential reward (i.e., cost savings, improved service, greater efficiency). Approval will be granted if and when you convince management that the risk is worthwhile based on potential reward. Thus, using the budget as a means for communicating a risk/reward scenario is an effective method for making proposals to management.

   The same argument applies when you want to alter the scope of a project. For example, in the course of executing the project, you may discover a potential for greater benefits than anticipated in the original assignment. Using budgetary arguments to express the risk/reward scenario in proposing a broadened scope is an effective method of communication.

The Schedule as a Communication Tool

The schedule defines your project and should be shared with management to ensure that your definition conforms with theirs. When the project is broken down into phases, management has the opportunity to validate your direction and approve the proposed deadline. This not only defines what the project will achieve, it also demonstrates why you may need a longer deadline than the one proposed with the initial assignment.

The schedule is useful during later phases in conjunction with review meetings both to ensure that you are on the right course and to verify that the direction is the one that management still expects. It also can be used to explain why an original deadline needs to be extended.

Finally, the schedule improves your communication with the core team and helps to avoid delays. By identifying weak links and communicating with other departments and outside resources well in advance of critical dates, you avoid many problems later on.

Working with Department Managers

For relatively uncomplicated, short-term projects executed strictly within a single department, you have direct control over the time commitment and priorities of each team member. Because you are aware of departmental deadlines and workload variations, you can construct a working schedule that anticipates heavier than average volume and make adjustments as needed. You also are able to balance departmental and project demands on the basis of your knowledge of each, as well as your knowledge of the different abilities among departmental staff members. The ability to control both departmental and project priorities gives you maximum control.

Your communication skills are tested, though, when you have to coordinate your project schedule with the requirements of other departments. A common complaint from managers is, "You didn't tell me in time." Regardless of the cause—deadlines, time management problems, or commitment conflicts—the problem invariably returns to a lapse in communication. You can solve the majority of the problems you will encounter working with departments by remembering one key point: Your project will have the best chance of staying on schedule when you keep department managers informed at all times.

By applying a few basic rules of communication between departments, you can defuse the problems that beset all managers at one time or another: territorial attitude, power struggles, and—in cases where communication fails altogether—outright refusal to cooperate. Most of the time, a breakdown of cooperation arises not from political or personality problems, but from a severe failure in the communication link. If you have attempted to communicate only once, that may not be enough. People need reminding, so don't assume that a single message is adequate.

Figure 12-1 summarizes the following important rules for improving and maintaining communication with other departments:

▧ *Visit the other manager before you finalize the schedule.* From your point of view, it is apparent that your schedule has to go into effect as designed. For example, the deadline leaves little room for adjustment, and an employee from another department has been placed on your team by the company president. Why contact that department's manager, you think, when everything has been settled?

Figure 12-1. Outside department checklist.

1. Visit the other manager before you finalize the schedule.

2. Keep in touch while the project is under way.

3. Work with the manager to anticipate problems.

4. Remain as flexible as possible.

5. Confront the problems, not the people.

This approach will lead to problems. No matter how restricted you are by an imposed deadline, and no matter how little say you had in picking your team, you have to be prepared to accommodate your team member's manager. Plan to discuss your schedule with that manager before you finalize it. Take this approach: Ask for a meeting and present your initial schedule, explaining that it is only preliminary. Ask whether the proposed schedule will cause any conflict with the employee's recurring duties in the department. If there is a scheduling problem, work with the manager to resolve it.

■ ***Keep in touch while the project is under way.**** Continue keeping the lines of communication open, even after the initial meeting. Even when the manager agrees with your schedule, unexpected conflicts can and do come up.

You can avoid conflict by staying in touch with the department manager throughout the project period. A weekly status check may be all you need. A three-minute telephone discussion should be enough to double-check schedules. By working together, you and the department manager will be able to resolve any conflicts that arise, such as the manager being given a project to complete at the same time as yours. By staying in touch, you avoid the kinds of breakdowns that lead to serious conflicts, both work-related and personal.

■ ***Work with the manager to anticipate problems.**** In addition to the periodic review, look toward the end of your project. Point out the phases that will require an especially heavy time commitment, and make sure it won't present any conflicts in coming phases.

Most managers appreciate the consideration of being kept informed and will gladly work out any scheduling problems. It's only when you don't anticipate future problems that conflicts are going to arise, obscuring your priorities and jeopardizing your relationship with the manager.

■ ***Remain as flexible as possible.**** Remember that few departments can judge very far in advance the demands that will be placed on them from above. Even anticipating a single monthly cycle is difficult in some departments. It's frustrating when another manager affects your scheduling by pulling an employee out to work on other jobs. This is not necessarily because he or she is devious or disorganized; it may simply be characteristic of the department and its workload.

Stop and think whenever you find yourself about to say, "You told me this wouldn't be a problem." It probably was true at the time, but since then, the department's assignments, deadlines, and priorities have probably changed. Successful project managers stay on schedule and within budget to the extent possible, even when team members from other departments are pulled suddenly. You will have to shift duties to someone else or do the work yourself. Regardless of the obvious inconvenience, remain as flexible as possible when dealing with other managers.

▪ *Confront the problems, not the people.* In some cases, managers will seem unreasonable, unyielding, defensive, and uncooperative. They may resent having an employee removed from their jurisdiction to work on your project, and this can create an array of hostile reactions.

The territorial reaction is one form of "corporate neurosis." Refusing to tolerate it will not solve the problem; nor will confronting the manager directly, because that only aggravates the situation. Egos are at play, and no matter how strong a manager is, egos are fragile things. The best solution is to concentrate on the problem the reaction creates, not on getting distracted and involved with the personal aspects of the conflict.

When a manager resists your efforts to commit an employee, emphasize the schedule and the deadline. Ask the manager to suggest a solution that satisfies the departmental needs as well as the project needs. Avoid discussing the matter on a personal level; concentrate on executing the task.

Working with Other Department Employees

The communication challenge is not limited to managers. You could also face resistance from team members who come from other departments. Conflicts arise in three general areas:

1. ***Career priorities.*** Employees tend to identify their personal career paths—thus priorities—in terms of their departments, not outside projects. They do not always appreciate the potential advancement opportunities that can arise by taking part in projects outside of their departments, especially those managed by someone other than their immediate supervisor.

2. ***Temporary assignments.*** Because the project is temporary, it often will be viewed as nothing more than an inconvenience, a disruption, extra work. Since it isn't their "real" job, employees may come to your project with a negative attitude.

3. ***Supervisory problems.*** As manager of a project, you may have more than the usual degree of problems supervising someone from another department. One reason is that you cannot determine the quality of corporate life to the same degree as an immediate supervisor. When the project is over, the employee returns to the department.

To overcome these problems apply the same rules you use in dealing with managers of other departments. Be aware of team members' priorities and conflicts. As long as they are working on your project, they are in the difficult position of reporting to two people. Do all that you can to minimize the problems associated with this situation, rather than aggravating it.

Remember, your team members have to meet deadlines on two levels: those of their department and those of your project. Work with core team members to solve scheduling conflicts and to anticipate upcoming problems as well.

Once you discover an emerging problem with a schedule, take immediate steps to solve it. Never assume the attitude that "You're on my team; I expect you to meet all deadlines." Instead, sit down with the team member and work together to figure out how to get around the problem. Either reassign work or adjust your schedule.

The project schedule is your problem and your responsibility. So even when a team member can't deliver as promised, it's up to you to do something about it. You create a positive reputation as a project manager by establishing two-way loyalty—from the team by working together and meeting deadlines, and to the team by remaining as flexible as possible.

Since project leadership is limited when you work with employees from other departments, you also need to adjust your leadership style. If you are accustomed to supervising people only on the departmental level, you may run into problems applying the same standards—and expecting the same response—on your project. Team members from other departments will not relate to you as a permanent supervisor and will not act as department employees.

You may need to put considerable thought into how to alter your style. What works best on the particular project? The answer will vary. It depends on the attitude and support of the department manager, the clarity of the assignment from management, the size and scope of the project and the team, the project's complexity, the deadline, and all of the individuals involved.

For example, when your project is relatively small and short term, you can act rather informally with the entire team, even members loaned from another department. Keep the lines of communication open and ensure that everyone understands their role. For a longer-term project, you are likely to be sharing employee hours with the department. This situation requires structuring a daily or weekly schedule. Not only must the employee be given time to work on the project in those scheduled hours, but other team members and your time has to be free during those hours as well, because the team needs to work together. Thus, your supervisory style needs to be more flexible for projects, considering team members' schedules and training requirements.

Working with Outside Consultants

Your communication skills will be further tested if you need to work with an outside consultant. You will need to contend with the independence of that adviser as well as with the question of who is running the project.

Consultants are oriented toward projects because of the nature of their work. They often are retained specifically to head up a project, whether it is called a project or something else. Their work is temporary, usually relatively short term, and does not fit within the work guidelines or style of departments, which means you may run into problems and conflicts working with them. Their role should be clearly defined to avoid such problems. While you might view your role as project manager and the consultant a member of your resource team, the consultant may see the roles in reverse. This potential problem has to be anticipated and cleared up at the very beginning.

Example

A manager was assigned a project that required working with an outside consultant. From the first day, it was apparent that the consultant viewed his role as project manager. When the manager met with the vice president who made the initial assignment, she was told that her role was to act as liaison between the consultant and management. In fact, she was not the project manager. This changed her approach entirely.

This is an example of very poor communication from upper management. Whenever management is unclear about the roles of individuals in a project, it is inviting conflict. From a consultant's point of view, an internal manager can become a distraction and intrusion to executing a project. Because the consultant is an outsider, he has no scheduling conflicts. Consultants probably have their own resources and time frame for completing the project. They do not report to management in the same way as employees, so their attitude is vastly different. As a result, communication between manager and consultant is likely to be strained. If, in fact, you are assigned the role of project manager, the consultants you are working with must understand that their role is advisory, or conflict will characterize the entire relationship.

The problem arises in some cases because management is itself conflicted about the roles of the internal manager and the external consultant. Management recognizes the need for both in the project; however, it feels compelled to call the internal manager the "project manager" even though it depends on the consultant to actually pilot the project. In this situation, even if you hash out the problem directly with the consultant, you are likely to have problems getting a firm commitment of time from an outsider. Consultants are not going to respond to your internal authority, a fact that some managers have trouble understanding at first. The fact that consultants do not think like employees can cause problems, since your schedule depends on a coordinated effort with all team members and other resources. With this in mind, you may need to get the participation from a consultant as early as possible and work your schedule around that. If problems arise, be sure to communicate them to management as part of your periodic review.

Even though you are responsible for meeting the deadline for your project, management needs to understand that some delays are beyond your control. This rule applies whenever you work with other departments, and even more when you work with independent outside resources. You can deal with this problem by following these three general guidelines:

1. *Design your schedule so that the consultant is given an early deadline.* Whenever possible, ask for the work from an outside consultant earlier than your actual deadline. This is not always practical, since the consultant's participation may depend on completion of a particular phase. But as a general rule, any work that does not depend on other phases should be completed as early as possible. Of course, making this request does not ensure that you get the results when you ask for them. Remember, because consultants are independent, they do not have the same point of view about reporting to you as an employee would.

2. *Be prepared to complete the work without the consultant.* In some cases, you can execute the phase that management expects from a consultant without holding up your schedule. The consultant may have been retained because management believes an outsider's point of view will be superior to that of an insider. It is unfortunate but true that some people think the more you pay per hour, the higher the quality of the work, even though that is not necessarily the truth. You and your core team may be able to get the work done with little or no problem. When this is the case, be sure to advise management that the work was completed internally—not to undo the relationship between the consultant and management, but to keep open the lines of communication. If you do the work with your internal team to remain on deadline, that is important information that management needs.

3. *Accept the delay as being beyond your control.* You cannot control the consultant's schedule, nor can you enforce a deadline. That is a reality. And you cannot always work around the consultant, either. You sometimes have to accept a delay, not only of a phase the consultant is responsible for completing, but as a consequence for the entire project. Once you realize that the project will be delayed as a result, inform management at once.

Weak Links in Communication

Weak links in scheduling and execution of tasks are obvious. They can be spotted easily as points where phases begin and end, or where the work process moves from one area of responsibility to another. A weak link in communication is a little more difficult to spot, but it can have an equally serious effect on the smooth operation of your project.

Such a weak link occurs whenever you have to communicate with someone outside your team, or even when information has to be conveyed within the core team, between individuals or subgroups. Effective communication, ensured by your careful oversight, is the best way to overcome communication weak links. There are five primary areas where the potential problem of communication weak links can occur:

1. *Team Member to Team Member.* Any time a team member needs to discuss the work of the project with another individual, another subgroup, or an outside resource, a communication weak link is possible. Even a one-day delay resulting because someone is waiting for an answer to a question is a potentially serious weak link. It throws the schedule off by one day, a problem that becomes cumulative if it happens frequently. Identify such weak links and look for them; also ask your core team members to advise you when their work is delayed because they are waiting for information from someone else.

2. *Manager to Team Member.* Whenever you talk to a team member, there is the possibility that you will create a weak link. You have to be sure that assignments are understood and that deadlines are specific. If you do not communicate clearly, work will not be done correctly or in a timely manner. Thus, it will have to be revised, meaning delays. It pays to make sure that every communication from you to a team member is clear in all respects.

3. *Manager to Outside Department Manager.* Another weak link occurs when you communicate with the manager of another department—either as a resource for your project or because a member of your team reports to that manager. You depend on cooperation from that manager to stay on schedule, so your communication skills are essential. You need to convey information clearly in any discussion of this type and be alert to the personal conflicts and attitudes you may encounter. Because that manager has a conflicting set of priorities, you must work out any differences to avoid delays.

4. *Manager to Outside Resource.* No matter how urgent your deadlines or how important the project is to your company, you should expect to have problems getting a timely response from an outside resource. Consultants, vendors, other divisions, and government agencies all have one thing in common: They do not report to you. Their priorities are not the same as yours, so your urgency about deadlines won't always be shared. This is a significant potential weak link. The solution is effective and careful communication. Don't wait until a deadline is pending to ask for outside information; anticipate delays and plan ahead so that the work will be there on time.

5. *Manager to Executive.* Once you are given a project assignment, your first task should be to ensure that you and management are in complete agreement. What is the purpose and desired end result? You may be able to meet a schedule and budget effectively, but if the outcome is not what management expected, then what is the point? You need to check with the people who gave you the assignment to ensure that you are doing what they expect. Unfortunately, an executive may not always communicate effectively; so you need to ask for clarification and definition to make sure the project is what you think it is.

Another potential problem arises when the executive changes your assignment after you have begun. This could even occur without your knowledge. For example, a decision is made by the board, but priorities change and no one tells you. The solution is to continue making periodic reports concerning schedule, budget, and overall progress. If a change has occurred, it is the executive's responsibility to inform you; the periodic report may serve as a reminder.

How Flowcharting Helps

The communication challenge exists on every level and stays with you throughout your project. It cannot be solved in isolation during the initial definition phase and then abandoned. Your role as controller and leader requires ongoing, unending communication—to dissolve weak links, soothe conflict, and revise your schedule when necessary.

Although primarily designed to serve as a working document for team members, your network diagram also works as an aid to effective communication—on all levels. For example, when discussing an upcoming schedule conflict for team members with their department manager, you can use the network diagram to work out reassignment, change the timing of a phase, or change work sequences. If the network diagram is too complex for this purpose, it could inhibit communication rather than help. If numerous concurrent phases will be under way during the problematical time, anyone not accustomed to using horizontal flowcharts could be confused by its design. In these cases, create a simplified top-to-bottom variation of the network diagram. This is more familiar to most people, and it will help in communicating the problems with isolated segments—whether phases or a segment of a longer phase.

Besides flowcharting tasks and identifying their deadlines, time factors can also be expressed with the use of flowcharts. For example, an upcoming deadline can be placed on paper in flowchart form, making it easier to work with another manager to identify possible ways to resolve conflict.

Flowcharts help other people to visualize the complexity of a project. They are effective for pointing out weak links, especially those arising out of scheduling conflicts between your project and a department. They help, too, when communicating with an outside resource. A consultant may not respond to your explanation about deadlines, but demonstrating the broader view of a project on a flowchart shows the consultant's role in the bigger picture. Because your job is to coordinate the efforts of many people and ensure multiple interim deadlines, the flowchart can clarify your point in ways that would not be possible in a face-to-face discussion.

The flowchart also paints a picture of the overall responsibility for managing a project. No one is going to appreciate all of the things you need to do without extra information, because people tend to understand what you say only to the degree that it affects them. If you simply state, "This is a tough job; I have to monitor the efforts of several people at the same time," that does not convey the real complexity of your role. The flowchart, however, shows people what you are up against, and how their role affects the whole schedule.

Meetings with Outside Resources

You will need to meet with your team, with the executive who assigns the project, and with outside resources—at the onset of the project and possibly while the project is under way. The meetings should be short and carefully limited in agenda, or you will spend so much time in discussion that the project will be delayed unreasonably.

Meetings with outside resources or department managers should be held primarily to anticipate problems and solve them. Your agenda should be designed with six goals in mind, as listed below and summarized in Figure 12-2.

1. *Express the goals of the project.* Never forget the ultimate goals of your project. You must state these goals more than once to remind outside resources what you are trying to achieve. Keeping the

Figure 12-2. Agenda when meeting with outsiders.

1. Express the goals of the project.

2. Explain the level of team commitment you need.

3. Specify deadlines for phases and final completion.

4. Identify critical phases.

5. Point out likely problem areas.

6. Agree on priorities for the project.

goal at the forefront of your discussion helps avoid sidetracking your agenda, and it also is an effective method for confronting problems, defusing arguments, and avoiding conflict. A goal orientation keeps discussions on track.

2. *Explain the level of team commitment you need.* You may face a confrontation with a department manager concerning the time requirements of an employee. The best response is not to argue about whose priorities are higher, but to explain the time demands of the project. You have a number of alternatives: reassignment, schedule adjustment, or extended deadlines, for example. The problem should never be derailed by making it an argument between two managers. Promote a joint effort and a professional approach to solve mutual problems with everyone's needs in mind.

3. *Specify deadlines for phases and final completion.* Avoid surprises when dealing with departments and other outside resources. If you face the argument, "You didn't tell me," either you didn't communicate a deadline or, if you did, the message did not get through. The solution is to base communications around the interim and final deadlines and emphasize them frequently.

4. *Identify critical phases.* Emphasize which deadlines are the least flexible, thus pivotal to your schedule. In this way you will improve your chances for staying on schedule throughout the project. These deadlines are the ones that have to be met before any additional work can proceed, and they often are the greatest weak links in your schedule. Convey this information to everyone concerned so that your requirements are known well in advance.

5. *Point out the likely problem areas.* Don't wait for someone else to discover problems. Anticipate them and then verbalize your concerns. The project manager's job is to look for problems before they occur. Department managers will appreciate your attention to detail when the problem affects them as well. For example, you might say, "During this phase, I will depend on the employee from your department. But I think it is scheduled during the high-volume period in your department's cycle." This gives both of you the opportunity to work out the problem before a deadline is upon you. It helps eliminate a scheduling problem and also improves your working relationship with the other manager.

6. *Agree on priorities for the project.* Some project managers try to meet deadlines and work toward an atmosphere of teamwork and cooperation, only to be faced with unending conflict on many levels: between team members, with outside resources, and with department managers. This problem arises because the priorities of the project were never expressed clearly or coordinated with others. The solution is to work on that all-important coordination of your priorities and the priorities of others.

Once you get people working together, the communication process works quite well. It is largely a matter of definition. However, in some projects the perceptions of various people and departments are at odds to the point that conflict is continuous. For example, your priority may be to gather information quickly, even if it means putting more people on the job; someone else's priority might be to reduce expenses. Whose priority should rule?

These are the kinds of difficult questions that have to be addressed. Solutions can, in fact, come in the form of compromise. Leave nothing unexplained or else wrong assumptions will fill in the gaps. If you expect to get any cooperation at all, it is up to you to explain what you are doing and what you need.

Running the Meeting

You might view meetings as usually being long, drawn-out exercises in discussion, leading to little in the way of results or decisions. Or you may view them simply as inefficient ways to get things done. However, a well-organized and controlled meeting—especially a short one—can improve communication and efficiency on all levels.

Your first task is to control the scope and time of the meeting in three ways:

1. *Invite only those people who are absolutely essential to the agenda.* The more people in your meeting, the more difficult it will be to stay on the subject or to get anything done.

2. *Limit the time.* If your meeting runs too long, you won't achieve the desired results.

3. *Set meeting goals yourself.* Write out an agenda—not just by topics but also by goals. What do you hope to accomplish in your meeting? People should be able to read the agenda and know exactly what is going to take place.

Next, you need to get your message across to attendees—whether team members, department managers, executives, consultants, or others. You maintain control of the meeting by moving through your agenda as quickly as possible and ensuring that decisions are made and actions assigned (with specific deadlines for completion). Some projects are helped with periodic five-minute team meetings, which are used to discuss the week's assignments. Other meetings can be called for specific conflicts and other problems. Remember to make use of communication tools during your meeting, including:

■ *The agenda.* The agenda itself is a powerful communication tool, if used properly. Each agenda item can be listed with a start/stop time or the number of minutes set aside for discussion. Limit the meeting by being as specific as possible, and then keep to the agenda. Any business that comes up that isn't on the agenda can be discussed one-on-one after the meeting has ended.

■ *Simplified flowchart.* Many people have problems understanding something as complex and detailed as the network diagram. They relate more easily to a traditional format top-to-bottom flowchart. This is a useful visual aid for discussion of isolated phases or work segments.

■ *Gantt chart.* To explain scheduling problems on a broad basis, the Gantt chart is the most effective visual aid. This is especially true when communicating with executives or outside resources who do not need to see the detailed breakdown by area of responsibility, but will be interested in overall scheduling questions.

■ *Network diagram.* For team meetings, the network diagram is probably the most effective visual aid. If you expect problems in the near future, the diagram is a practical format for a discussion of the problem and possible solutions.

· · · · · · · · · · ·

In all phases of project management, the degree to which you are able to communicate your priorities determines the success of your efforts. Identifying problems well in advance, expressing your understanding of someone else's priorities, and confronting issues rather than people are all attributes of effective communicators and successful project managers.

Your ability to overcome communication problems affects your role as employee and manager in a larger sense than your role as project manager. The next chapter discusses project management and its potential positive effects on your career.

WORK PROJECT

1. Explain the communication challenge on three levels:
   a. The assignment
   b. Working with other departments
   c. Working with outside resources

2. Describe at least three ideas for improving communication when working with other departments.

3. List at least three goals to include on your agenda for a project meeting with another department.

Project Management and Your Career

Share your vision of success with your employees. It's something they can win if they put out the effort. They'll get excited about success when they know you're excited.

—NICHOLAS V. IUPPA, AUTHOR OF *MANAGEMENT BY GUILT*—

"I think our manager is burned out," one project team member told another.

The second one agreed: "I've noticed that he's been a bit short-tempered lately."

"That's not what I mean," the first one said. "Yesterday, he sent me down to the lunchroom to get him a cup of coffee."

"What's wrong with that?"

"Instead of just giving me a list, he drew out his instructions on a network diagram."

Who gets promoted in your company? Is it the person who is merely capable, doesn't make waves, and survives without upsetting the delicate balance of the corporate culture? Or is it the person who excels?

Because survivors are not risk takers, they are eventually overlooked. They may do well initially, but in the long term, it is the exceptional manager who receives promotions and gains a profitable and fulfilling career. Whether your performance as a department manager is exceptional or only average, if you also manage projects you have the chance to exceed beyond the "average" category.

In many departments, budgets, staff, recurring tasks, and other factors limit your freedom to express and demonstrate your skills to their greatest potential. You may be working full time just to maintain the minimum requirements of the job. You may face few opportunities to even have your abilities put to the test. But when a project comes along, that could be your chance to not only develop your leadership skills, but show management what you can do in a high-profile project. Managing a complex job and skillfully delivering the result on time will get management's attention.

An Organizational Science

A large part of your success as a project manager depends on your abilities to organize and define. In comparison, the actual work is not difficult. In fact, the better you organize and define all aspects of your project, the easier it is to execute tasks.

Organizing the project requires several leadership actions on your part, including:

■ **Defining the purpose and goals of the project.** Getting to the point of understanding between yourself and the person giving you the assignment can take a great deal of effort on your part. Don't expect the definition to be handed to you. Many people, including executives, have difficulty explaining precisely what they want. It is all too easy to take on an assignment without having a clear idea of what it is supposed to achieve. Your first organizational challenge is to ask the right questions at the time of assignment.

■ **Organizing a schedule.** Once a schedule is completed, it should look like a fairly simple document. Each phase is broken down and defined; deadlines are specific; and tasks are assigned to team members. But a complex and lengthy project demands a far greater level of organizational skill in the beginning. You need to coordinate time demands for each phase while anticipating potential problems. You must also be aware of time restrictions for each of your team members. Thus, you need to look far ahead, through to the end of the project, in order to organize the schedule realistically.

■ ***Developing a team approach.*** Your ability to lead the project team effectively depends on how well your team works together. This does not take place without strong, motivated, and focused leadership. Simply assigning people to the team doesn't make it a working team. The better you organize every aspect of the project and define what you need and expect, the easier it will be to develop the team. A team does not begin functioning properly right away; development of the team is an ongoing process that lasts as long as the project.

■ ***Resolving conflicts.*** Invariably, the pressures associated with working against deadlines and cooperating with a variety of internal and external resources will create conflict at some point, perhaps several times. Many of these conflicts relate to scheduling between recurring department duties and the demands of the project; others may arise from disagreements or competition between team members. As project manager, you need to be ready to act as mediator and diplomat to avoid the kinds of difficulties that are unavoidable whenever people work together.

■ ***Keeping the lines of communication open.*** As project manager, you must continually define, redefine, and modify. You also need to train team members, cooperate with department managers, enlist help from outside resources, and reassure top management. Your project team does not operate in isolation, so your task is to function as organizer and operator of a network with conflicting interests and priorities.

■ ***Meeting budgets and deadlines.*** As the organized project manager, you need to review status daily. That means tracking the budget and schedule and looking for any sign of variances or delays, and then taking action to correct problems. You monitor each phase as it proceeds, with an eye to the immediate deadline as well as the final deadline. The tools you need for this purpose include the Work Breakdown Structure (WBS), Critical Path Method (CPM), Gantt chart, and network diagram.

■ *Training and supervising team members.* While the project is under way, you must supervise team members directly. Some people may not know how to execute a task, for example. It is often assumed that team members know how to do their tasks without supervision, and that is a mistake. Don't overlook the most obvious function of all—helping team members understand their immediate assignments.

Attributes of Project Leadership

Achieving the many organizational objectives of project management places demands on you and your leadership skills. In some departments, "participative" management is not always possible or practical. Departments are not best run in a democratic manner. In projects, however, it is more likely that team members can be given the freedom to express ideas and contribute to the project in creative ways, even to take on part of the leadership role.

The team relationship is ever-changing and has to be altered with each individual. While you may be familiar with the relational aspects of managing a department, you may need to adjust for the project. Your project management skills are put to best use when:

■ *You understand and practice the team approach.* Some people endorse participative management in concept, but don't really understand how it works. To succeed in project management, you need to make the best use of the team. Creating a team by picking members is just the first step; you also need to allow the team the flexibility to excel, which usually means relaxing the kinds of controls you employ in the department.

■ *You apply a standard that is different from the one used in your department.* Some very capable department managers struggle with projects because they do not make an easy transition from running a permanent department. Project management is far different in most of its aspects, so a completely different approach is required to make it work. You need to remain in control, of course, but you also need to encourage a more democratic approach than you can in your department.

     ▨ *You can organize a multiple effort.* On a complex project, team members operate on several phases and levels at the same time. You need to organize the concurrent effort, supervise everyone, and monitor schedule and budget—all at the same time. You may also need to supervise and train team members as they move through phases. On top of all this, you probably need to continue running your department as well.

     ▨ *You are flexible.* Even the best-defined plans change for a variety of reasons, most of which are beyond your immediate control. Be prepared for unexpected change—in your schedule, resources, and even in the definition of the project itself.

     ▨ *You communicate well with everyone.* You may be deeply involved in the hands-on work of the project, supervising team members, and monitoring the schedule and budget. But you remain responsible for keeping open the lines of communication on all levels—between team members and with departments, outside resources, and top management.

Taking Charge

Living up to the standards of project management success may seem to demand a superhuman effort. The requirements of supervision and communication—both of which are needed in order to execute the project as an exception to your normal routine—place considerable pressure on you. However, the solution is not to put in more hours or effort, but to work to define your goals and then execute them. To achieve this in an orderly and realistic manner, measure results not in hours spent, but in organizational skills and their application.

Staying in control in your department calls for a firm hand. You succeed as a project manager when you adopt a more flexible leadership style—without giving up the strength of leadership. Your precise style in leading your project team should be modified based on at least four general variables:

1. *The makeup of the team.* With a fairly small team consisting of employees from your department, your leadership style can remain constant. This is the easiest form of team structure to work with, because there are no outside resources with their inherent independence and conflicting priorities to complicate matters. But that is not how things always work out. As soon as the team expands beyond your department, your style needs modification.

2. *Scope of the project.* Some projects are meant to function only as committees, put together to investigate, compile data, and report. Other projects are more action-oriented, organized to make significant changes. Projects may be short term or last many months. The style you employ with your team has to be based on the purpose, scope, and duration of each project.

3. *Cooperation from other departments.* We would all like to believe that other managers will cheerfully cooperate with our efforts. In practice, this does not always occur. Thus, your management style has to be flexible so that you can cooperate, negotiate, compromise, and adjust to varying levels of response.

4. *Time demands.* You may need to complete a project under extreme time constraints. In some companies, this is the norm; everything is critical and work proceeds on a continual emergency basis. The greater the pressure to finalize a project, the less luxury you enjoy to experiment with management styles; the "style" has to be to rush the project through.

How you take charge of a project depends largely on your personal experience. As you move through the process of managing projects, you will discover what works and what does not. The circumstances unique to one project do not apply to another.

Eliminating Common Problems

Even when you organize and lead your projects well, you may find yourself running into the same problems time and again. Learning how to resolve these difficulties improves your chances of becoming more effective in your project management role. Ten common problems you are likely to face are outlined in Figure 13-1. Each is discussed in depth here:

1. ***The team doesn't work well together.*** When you struggle to create a team but don't succeed, first examine your own management

Figure 13-1. Ten common problems for project managers.

1. The team doesn't work well together.

2. Other managers resist having their employees recruited to your team.

3. Management skills that work in the department don't seem to work on the project.

4. The goals of the project are not well defined.

5. Top management changes the scope of the project after it has started.

6. Communication with top management while the project is under way is not effective.

7. The schedule is difficult to control.

8. Deadlines are not being met, and projects are completed late.

9. Project budgets don't work, resulting in expense overruns.

10. There is no time for overview or control.

style. Do you offer team members the chance to participate and take control over their area of responsibility? Or do you discourage them from speaking out, offering ideas or alternatives, or suggesting changes? Teams work best when you encourage participation and then follow up on it with your actions.

The problem can also be caused by the very diversity among your core team. The involvement of people from several different departments can be detrimental to the development of real team action. The more people are involved and the more diverse their backgrounds, the greater your difficulty is going to be in getting people to cooperate and think and act as a real team.

2. *Other managers resist having their employees recruited to your team.* You face a formidable task in getting cooperation from other department managers—no matter how diplomatically you approach them or how well you define and explain the project. To solve this problem, you must convince other managers that you will respect their priorities—and their territory.

3. *Management skills that work in the department don't work on the project.* Be aware of the important differences between departmental management and project management. You need to employ different forms of supervision and leadership with each. In fact, the skills that work most effectively in your department tend to interfere with team participation, so strive to develop an entirely different approach to supervising a project team.

4. *The goals of the project are not well defined.* Your first responsibility is to ensure that the goals of the project are clearly and specifically spelled out. You may have to push to get the assignment clarified before you are able to develop and explain its goals. It often is true that even the executive who gives you the assignment doesn't really know what he or she expects from the project. Only when you have clear definition can you approach your task as a science.

5. *Top management changes the scope of the project after it has started.* Unfortunately, priorities change. You cannot safely assume that a project assigned today will remain valid by its deadline.

Chronic changes in project assignment are symptoms of weak leadership, and in that case there is little that you can do to work effectively in seeing the project through to its end. However, even in the best of environments, a particular project can become obsolete, requiring modification or even a complete revision. Be flexible so that you can adjust to unexpected changes in the nature of the assignment itself.

6. *Communication with top management while the project is under way is not effective.* How do you handle the problem of poor communication with top management? Even when you make the effort to keep the lines open, management does not always keep you in the loop about changing priorities.

You cannot force management to improve communication skills. You can only present status reports, ask for continuing definition, and convey information. If you cannot get an executive to take time for a brief meeting, chances are communication will be poor no matter what steps you take. You may find that management fails to respond to your suggestions or requests, does not confirm project goals, and offers little or no support. Nothing is worse than this situation, because you are operating in a vacuum. When you present your final work on the project, you are likely to be told, "This is not what I wanted."

Management wants to support you, of course, to maintain morale and reduce unnecessary expenditure of staff time. You can resolve problems of this nature most of the time by making an extra effort to get consensus from management about the project and what it is supposed to accomplish.

7. *The schedule is difficult to control.* Coordinating the efforts of many subgroups and individuals within a limited time frame is always a struggle. Examine the methods you use to monitor your schedule and to convey vital information to team members. A nicely detailed network diagram is an effective tool for ensuring that team members have a good perspective on the project and their roles. Most scheduling problems result from lack of enough detail in the schedule document itself.

8. *Deadlines are not being met, and projects are completed late.* Even with the best procedures for schedule control, and even

when team members work well together, you will not always be able to meet phase deadlines or deliver the project by deadline.

Your schedule may be unrealistic, especially if imposed on you from above. It may be necessary to accept delays in order to ensure quality and accuracy, or to increase the size of the project team. If management has given you an unrealistic deadline, you need to bring this fact to its attention and request a modification. Either the schedule needs to be changed or the staff budget increased. Failing either of these actions, your project will either be late or done in a hurry. A realistic completion time for the project is always defined by the scope of the job, and that cannot be known accurately until it has been mapped out. Thus, the very situation in which a deadline is imposed before the project has been planned out makes no sense. The best you can do in this situation is to go back to management with your schedule and try to discuss alternatives, preferably including an extended deadline.

9. *Project budgets don't work, resulting in expense overruns.* In your preoccupation with the schedule, it's easy to overlook the importance of the budget. Realistically, the schedule is the key to running a project. However, top management is likely to be more concerned with whether you are exceeding a budget, even an arbitrary one. Budgets have to be monitored with great care because it's the nature of management to judge effectiveness in terms of spending levels.

Unfortunately, many people in business—including executives—do not understand the purpose of budgeting. While it should serve as a standard for measuring actual results, the budget often becomes established as an absolute, and any unfavorable variances imply a failure somewhere along the way, usually with the project manager. While this practice is unfair and unrealistic, it may also be the status quo in your organization. Budget variances arise for one of three reasons: The original budget was unrealistic; expenses are not being controlled well enough; or most significantly, when the budget was developed, it did not anticipate the real expense of the project. If a budget was imposed on your project before its scope was understood, then you face the all-too-common problem of budgets being misused. You are expected to conform to a budget that has nothing to do with the expense levels you face. Your best solution is to compare realities to the budget and explain unfavorable variances in the context that makes sense: The budget was not adequate for the project.

10. ***There is no time for overview or control.*** You may find yourself committed so heavily to project tasks and supervision (not to mention ongoing departmental duties) that you don't have time to monitor schedules and budgets.

No matter how busy you are, monitoring and controlling are your primary responsibilities as a project manager. Although you have to fill many roles—trainer, supervisor, leader, communicator, and morale officer—your primary job remains pilot. The project network is complex and can't run on its own. You may need to delegate tasks to others to free up your time for this all-important function. Avoid the mistake of getting so involved in the details of the project that you don't have time to step back and make sure you're on course.

Maximizing Your Skills

As you gain experience managing projects, your career possibilities will expand as well. A top management team that is cognizant of its resources will recognize ability and reward it. Projects are an exceptional forum for demonstrating your leadership abilities.

In addition to developing the skills required for effective project management, set career goals based on the abilities you develop as a project manager. Your top-five goals may include, for example:

1. ***Acquiring a reputation as a skilled, effective project manager.*** Be aware of the importance of reputation to your career. Reliability is a crucial attribute. Once you are seen as reliable, you will be seen as a candidate for promotion. Become a skilled project manager by practicing the techniques that make the process work. Become an effective project manager by keeping goals in mind at all times, working to meet deadlines, supporting your team, and working well with all resources, whether internal or external.

2. *Meeting deadlines.* Some people accept the fact that deadlines are not taken seriously most of the time. Don't allow yourself to think this way. View deadlines in absolute terms, and strive to meet or beat them without fail. If you never miss a reasonable deadline, management will view you as professional and reliable. If deadlines are not going to be met, communicate that information as soon as you know and propose solutions to management. People at the top will view you as serious and responsible in that case.

3. *Staying within budget.* The budget, like the schedule, is often misused or not taken seriously. Few people use budgets as a means for comparing results against a standard. Look at budgets as a means for defining and controlling your project. Remember that success within a company often is measured by how much or how little is spent within departments or in projects. Your budget should be a realistic expression of what the project should cost. The degree to which you are able to come in under budget will be used by top management as a measurement of your effectiveness.

4. *Producing and delivering the desired result.* Once you have achieved a clear definition of your project's purpose, you should know exactly what management expects in the way of results. As long as you keep communicating about your progress toward the project's goal, you will succeed. Produce and deliver the desired result, and management will view you as a results-oriented manager. That is, after all, the job of the project manager.

5. *Resolving conflicts.* Conflicts—whether involving mere scheduling problems or the more difficult personality clash—might seem a trivial matter in the bigger scheme of things. But your ability to resolve conflicts may end up being the most important attribute of project management. In some volatile situations, conflict defines the project environment. It demands energy, diplomacy, and a sincere effort to address everyone's concerns to defuse conflict.

. . . .

Career opportunities within your company are going to be filled by individuals whom management believes can fill the need. Job skills are mundane attributes compared to the skills you gain by experiencing project management and completing the project successfully. You can demonstrate your value to the organization by your ability to provide strong leadership, resolve conflicts, manage a multitask schedule, communicate on all levels, work with other managers, inspire a diverse team to work together, and produce the desired result within a deadline.

As a project manager, the project itself is the opportunity to demonstrate your best qualities, to a greater extent than you can do as a department manager. When you accept a project assignment, remember that management will develop its perception of your capabilities (or limitations) based on your performance in that role, the results you generate, and the conflicts you are able to resolve quietly and effectively. You don't need a high profile, just a consistent and successful record based on producing results.

You'll know you are on the right track when management comes to you with their most difficult, complex jobs. That tells you that your hard work has paid off, because management asks for you when it needs a job done professionally.

WORK PROJECT

1. Describe at least three types of leadership action required to organize a project.

2. Explain at least three skills you need to master to succeed as a project manager.

3. List two or more variables that will affect your project leadership style.

Finding the Best Project Management Software

Many software programs can be put to use online or through purchase. Some are free, and others require purchase or online collaboration. Before purchasing any system, review and check it through reviews in one of the many software magazines or online sources.

Following is a list of some of the programs you can find online:

Artemis	http://www.aisc.com/
Basecamp	http://basecamphq.com/
Business Process Manager	http://www.planview.com
Central Desktop	http://www.centraldesktop.com
Clarizen	http://www.clarizen.com
Collanos	http://www.collanos.com
Computer Associates	http://www.ca.com
Copper Project	http://www.copperproject.com
Daptiv	http://www.daptiv.com
Easy Projects	http://www.easyprojects.net
EnterPlicity	http://www.teaminteractions.com

evisioner	http://www.evisioner.com
FastTrack Schedule	http://www.aecsoftware.com/products/fasttrack
GanttProject	http://ganttproject.biz
Gatherspace	http://www.gatherspace.com
Genius Inside	http://www.geniusinside.com/web/website.nsf
InLoox	http://www.inloox.com
Kplato	http://koffice.org/kplato
LiquidPlanner	http://www.liquidplanner.com
MicroPlanner X-Pert	http://www.microplanning.com
Microsoft Project	http://www.microsoft.com/en-us/project
Minuteman	http://www.minuteman-systems.com
OmniPlan	http://www.omnigroup.com/applications/omniplan
OpenAir	http://www.openair.com
OpenMind Business	http://www.matchware.com/en/products/openmind/default.htm
Open Plan Professional	http://www.welcom.com
OpenProj	http://www.projity.com
Planisware	http://www.planisware.com
Planner Suite	http://www.plannersuite.com
Primavera P6	http://www.primavera.com
Project Insight	http://www.projectinsight.net
Project Kickstart	http://www.projectkickstart.com
Project.net	http://www.project.net
ProjectPartner	http://www.projectpartner.com
ProjectPier	http://www.projectpier.org
Projectplace	http://www.projectplace.com
ProWorkFlow	http://www.proworkflow.com
RationalPlan	http://www.rationalplan.com
RiskyProject	http://www.intaver.com
SaaS VPMi	http://www.vcsonline.com
Santexq	http://www.santexq.com
SharpForge	https://sharpforge.org/p/SharpForge.aspx
SmartDraw	http://www.smartdraw.com

TaskJuggler	http://www.taskjuggler.org
Task Manager	http://www.taskmanagementsoft.com
Teamwork	http://www.twproject.com
Trac	http://trac.edgewall.org
Track+	http://www.trackplus.com
Tracker Suite	http://www.acentre.com
ValleySpeak	http://www.valleyspeak.com
ViewPath	http://www.viewpath.com
web-based-software	http://www.project-management-software.org
Wrike	http://www.wrike.com
Zoho Projects	http://projects.zoho.com/jsp/home.jsp

Appendix

Work Project Answers

It is not the answer that enlightens, but the question.

—EUGÈNE IONESCO—

Chapter 1

1. Project tasks and departmental routines can usually be distinguished clearly from one another in four ways:

a. Project tasks are exceptions to normal responsibilities or the range of functions of a department. Routines, by comparison, are defined by the scope of the department itself.

b. Project activities are related to one another in some manner. Routines are related to the function of the department.

c. Project goals and deadlines are specific and finite. Routine goals and deadlines tend to be more general, cyclical, and perpetual in nature.

d. A project's end result is identified specifically. Routines are undertaken as part of the course of departmental work.

2. The three constraints for every project are the result, budget, and time. Project managers must ensure that the result is well defined before beginning to work on the project. They must devise, monitor, and control the budget; and they must ensure that interim and final deadlines are met.

    3. The *definition* phase of the project includes four segments:

    a. Determining the project's purpose
    b. Identifying tasks
    c. Developing a schedule
    d. Creating a budget

The *control* phase has five parts:

    a. Putting together the project team
    b. Coordinating work during each phase
    c. Monitoring progress
    d. Taking action to correct unfavorable variances or avoid scheduling delays
    e. Completing the project on time

    Both the definition and control phases require careful organization. Without either, the project cannot be completed in time or within budget, and the desired result will not even be defined.

Chapter 2

    1. Six Sigma has two different aspects. As a system for managing projects and developing quality control, it describes the steps needed to move through the project. As a part of the organizational culture, Six Sigma enables people of all ranks to adopt an enlightened view of responsibility, teamwork, and effective improvement within the organization.

    2. Weak links may include poor input data, flaws in processing, or lack of control over output. In other words, they can take place at any part of the process. However, if you focus on any place in the process where steps move between people or departments, you will locate the majority of weak links. This is where they are most likely to occur.

3. DMAIC (define, measure, analyze, improve, control) describes the methodical approach to project management. You *define* the team, the process owner, the goal of the project, and the steps in the process. You *measure* by data collection and defect prevention. You *analyze* sources, processes, data, resources, and communications. You *improve* with alternative solutions, experimentation, and planning for future change. And, finally, you *control* with specific quality control steps, standardization, and the way in which you respond when defects occur.

Chapter 3

1. The direct team structure involves contact between the project manager and each team member. This is an appropriate organizational structure when you are working with a small team and there is no need for an intermediate reporting level. The direct team structure is simple and reduces bureaucracy. Direct contact also improves team coordination and communication.

2. The organizational team structure is appropriate for larger teams. As project manager, you'll need to delegate responsibility to middle ranks; otherwise, you'll spend too much time on the details of the project and won't have time for important monitoring and control functions. Actual supervision over phases is delegated to assistants in order to free up your time for oversight.

3. The agenda for the initial project meeting should set a tone and create a participative environment. The agenda may include:

a. *A List of Problems the Team Will Solve.* Your initial list may be expanded through discussions with team members.
b. *Solutions the Team Should Reach.* Again, team participation can increase the overall quality of problem solving through the group's identification of additional or alternative solution paths.
c. *Information the Team Needs.* You may be aware of several possible sources for raw data or completed reports useful to your team, and the team members may be able to offer additional ideas that could save time and effort.

d. *Initial Assignments.* You probably start out with a fair idea of who should execute specific tasks or phases. But remember, team members have recurring deadlines and tasks to complete as part of their departmental duties, and there could be a conflict. Team members might suggest shifting or sharing project tasks.

e. *Advance Planning.* Map out responsibilities for each phase of the project in advance, subject to modification later. At this point, your goal should be to ensure that the team is complete and that the team members appreciate the scope of the project.

Chapter 4

1. Having your project team imposed on you, rather than selecting its members on your own, is a difficult beginning to your project. When this occurs, consider these steps:

a. *Suggest a different approach.* Talk to the person who gave the assignment to you and explain why you believe it's essential that you are involved in selecting your team—subject to upper management's approval.

b. *Do your best with what you are given.* Even when your team is not the right team in your opinion, you still need to give it your best effort. If the decision has been finalized, there is little you can do to change matters.

c. *Give team members the chance to excel.* When you don't give someone the benefit of the doubt, you miss the chance to be surprised and to let that person develop and prove his or her skills.

d. *Request team members who work out well.* Ask for people on the next project who were especially valuable on your last one.

e. *Ask to take part in the selection process.* You may not be allowed to pick your team with complete independence, but a compromise is possible if management will listen to your ideas and recommendations.

 f. *Suggest that department managers be involved as well.*
The team member's immediate supervisor could be a valuable
participant in the selection process.

 2. An area of responsibility includes a range of tasks falling within
a defined skill level or emphasis. One employee may be especially
skilled in analysis, interpretation, or writing, for example. The area of
responsibility differs from the assignment of specific tasks in these ways:

 **a. *The project is defined not just by its phases but also by the
type of effort.*** Team members better understand the desired
end result when they are allowed to take responsibility over part
of the overall project.

 **b. *Areas of responsibility are matched to skills of individuals
or subgroups.*** You can achieve better results when you match
tasks to skills and strengths, rather than just giving out tasks to
a resource pool.

 c. *The area of responsibility approach provides incentives.* It
allows team members to assume a sense of ownership over a
phase or grouping of related tasks.

 3. The outside department is assumed to have higher priorities
than your project because:

 a. *You need the manager's support.* Be prepared to express
your appreciation for the department's priorities, and recognize
that assigning a member of that department to your project
team creates hardships for the department manager.

 **b. *The department's work is permanent, whereas the project
is only temporary.*** A project has a finite life, but the department's work continues month after month. From the employee's point of view, ongoing routines are higher priorities.

 **c. *Departmental tasks recur and often are tied to deadlines
within the monthly cycle.*** Thus, the work of the department is
likely to affect many other departments as well. Concede the
point that the department's work has to come first. Anticipate

problems as far in advance as possible and work to avoid conflicts in the schedule.

Chapter 5

1. The percentage-of-completion shows your estimate of each
phase's portion of the total, based on labor expenses. This is a valid
approach when labor represents most of your project budget. To calculate, divide the hours of each phase by total estimated project hours:

Phase	Hours	Percentage (%)	Cumulative Percentage (%)
1	28	10	10
2	63	24	34
3	76	29	63
4	97	37	100
Total	264	100%	

To calculate the dollar cost, multiply each team member's hourly rate
of pay by the budgeted hours in each phase:

Team Member	Hourly Cost	Phase 1	2	3	4
1	$20	$200	$300	$300	$500
2	15	120	120	90	180
3	18	0	270	450	360
4	9	0	180	180	225
5	10	100	50	100	150
Total		$420	$920	$1,120	$1,415

3. Nonlabor expenses can be budgeted on the percentage-of-
completion method, tied to labor. However, an adjustment is necessary
if and when nonlabor costs do *not* follow the labor trend closely. On
the assumption that expenses will follow the general trend of labor
expenditures, calculate each phase's expense levels by multiplying the
percentage completed by the total—in the example, the total of ex-

penses. Assuming a total in nonlabor expenses of $2,800, the budget would be calculated as follows :

Phase	Percentage (%)	Amount
1	10	$280
2	24	672
3	29	812
4	37	1,036
Total	100%	$2,800

Chapter 6

1. The following points are important when confronting delays:

a. *Every delay affects scheduling for the remainder of the project.* Thus, if the first five phases are delayed by two working days each, you are ten days off schedule for the final deadline.

b. *To meet your deadline, delays need to be absorbed in later phases.* It is unlikely that you will have the luxury of plenty of time since projects often are assigned with pressure for speedy completion. You need to plan for absorption of delays even when you have little or no scheduling flexibility.

c. *Though it's desirable to meet the final deadline, that is not practical if the outcome would be incomplete, inaccurate, or short of the desired result.* You need to balance the importance of the deadline against the quality of the outcome.

d. *Staying on schedule and meeting the final deadline is your job as project manager.* This means you must carefully track each and every phase—not only to avoid delays as they occur, but also to anticipate and prevent problems before they cause schedule delays.

2. Phases 1, 2, and 3 could be executed within the same time span. Even though it is important to define them as separate phases for the sake of clarity, they can be executed concurrently. The same approach will work for phases 5 and 6.

3. To eliminate delays, consider the following solutions:

a. Execute phases concurrently, even if your original plan called for consecutive scheduling. Look for instances where all or part of a phase can overlap another.

b. Double up the team's effort to absorb delays. This makes the most sense in later phases of the project as the final deadline approaches.

c. Begin preliminary steps on future phases to save time later.

d. Look for ways to speed up later phases, without sacrificing quality.

3. Delays can be eliminated in at least three ways. First, you can double up on processes that can be executed at the same time. There is not always a requirement that each phase has to wait until the previous one has been completed. Second, when the schedule falls behind, you can accelerate it by asking team members to put in more time to get back on schedule. Third, you can reduce future time constraints by seeking ways to speed up future steps in the schedule.

Chapter 7

1. Work Breakdown Structure (WBS) in outline form is a starting point for more detailed scheduling activity. WBS provides three important benefits:

a. *It allows you to identify responsibility by team member or subgroup.* Once the outline exists, specific phases can be assigned individually.

b. *It provides the means to control time on a detailed level.* From the outline, you can estimate time requirements for each phase and save time by identifying phases that can be worked concurrently.

c. *It helps identify weak links.* These are points where work and responsibility pass from one person or group to another, and where delays are most likely to occur.

2. Project management is well suited to automated processing, assuming you also follow these guidelines:

a. *Solve the problems of project management as a first step.* Don't make the mistake of believing that actual management can be replaced by automation.

b. *Identify recurring processes that might be better handled with an automated system.* Don't assume that all project management tasks will work well within a program. Some management functions have to be handled one-on-one and cannot be reduced to software solutions.

c. *Automate for processing and record-keeping efficiency.* Don't expect automation to replace your direct involvement with your team.

d. *Don't confuse project objectives and automation objectives.* The project schedule and budget are achieved by team effort, which can be aided and made more efficient with the right software.

e. *Don't change procedures to compensate for software limitations.* Remember, your priorities include getting the results you need. If a particular software program doesn't conform to what you need, then automation defeats your intended purpose.

f. *Develop practical and efficient systems for managing your project manually.* Then look for ways to improve efficiency, including automating aspects of the job that make sense, such as schedule charting, work assignments, and budgeting.

3. Setting rules for how you'll prepare your project's flowchart can clear up confusion when trying to represent a complex procedure in visual form. The following guidelines will help:

a. *The precedence method should always be used.* Every activity must be preceded by a logical activity or event.

b. *The activity and event paths have to make sense.* Every process contains a logical flow that's identified by (1) defining what an activity should achieve, (2) understanding what is needed to get to that point, and (3) knowing what has to come next.

    c. *An activity cannot occur until a preceding activity or event has been completed.* For example, action cannot just start up in the middle of a process without any connection to a prior activity or event.

    d. *Concurrent events have to be plotted, explained, and controlled with great care.* The team may be involved in two or more phases at the same time, which is a challenge to your organizational abilities.

    e. *Controlling weak links is the key to effective scheduling.* Concentrate on ensuring that delays do not occur at weak links and you will prevent the majority of likely schedule delays.

    f. *Decision points have to be flowcharted with great care to avoid confusion.* Accompany decision points with narrative explanations and supervise these points closely to ensure that workflow continues on schedule.

Chapter 8

1. An *activity* includes all of the action steps required within a phase, which consists of several activities. An *event* is the result or outcome that is developed from a series of activities. Remember these points about activities and events:

    a. The action of preparing a report is an activity; the report itself is an event.

    b. Receiving a report from another department is an event, which leads to a subsequent activity or series of activities.

    c. Any information received from the outside represents an event. For the purpose of flowcharting definition, the tangible item (e.g., report, raw data, records) is called an event, and what is done with that item is classified as an activity.

2. Vertical flowcharting may be a necessary step in defining the logical sequence of phases. However, this method provides little for scheduling control and has several flaws, including:

> a. *It lacks time requirement elements for each activity or phase.* The network diagram solves this problem by linking each activity to a time line.
>
> b. *There's no breakdown by area of responsibility.* The network diagram is a superior tool for orienting your team because it shows workflow for the entire project and by area of responsibility.
>
> c. *There's no breakdown of concurrent activity.* The Gantt chart is a better tool for visualizing how work can proceed and for showing overlapping phases.

3. Weak links are points in your schedule where delays are most likely to occur, usually as the consequence of poor communication. The weak link is the greatest threat to keeping your project on schedule. The network diagram helps you to identify and anticipate each weak link; it occurs whenever the activity link goes from one area of responsibility to another.

Chapter 9

1. Quality control and value often cross over. By reducing time requirements as part of quality control initiatives, for example, value is added to the overall process. However, value may exist on its own simply as a result of greater efficiency from improved processes, without adding quality. When value is created without improvements in quality, one danger may be a *loss* of quality due to more efficient (but more relaxed) internal controls.

2. Organizational morale defines how motivated team members will be and how cooperatively outside resources are going to react to your requirements and to your recommended changes. Low morale kills spirit and infects others, and it is fixed only by improved communication and honest dealings from top management as well as from managers up and down the chain of command. As project manager, overcoming low morale can be among the most daunting of tasks. It often requires that you focus on isolating pockets of team members to focus on immediate tasks and to ignore larger organizational problems.

3. Making suggestions at the start of your project for methods of measuring success is wise because it helps management and your team to set and reach goals. At the same time, flexibility is important because specific goals might change; so these established interim goals might change as the project develops and moves forward.

Chapter 10

1. This series of activities involves two team members, so it should be divided into two separate sections. One solution is to show the sequence of actions, divided by team members, as shown in Figure A-1.

2. Loops are points in the network diagram where decisions need to be made. They are divided into three general types:

   a. Verification loops ask questions that are answered with a "correct" or "incorrect" response. For example, an activity requires checking math on a worksheet. If correct, proceed to the next activity; if incorrect, go to the previous step and find and correct errors.

   b. A decision loop is answered with a "yes" or "no." For example, a rough draft of a form is submitted to the project manager for review. A "yes" response (i.e., approval) leads to the next activity. A "no" response (i.e., changes needed) leads the team member back to the drafting phase.

   c. A repetition loop is used when one activity is repeated several times. It is characterized by a response of "complete" or "not complete." For example, an activity calls for checking the work of three employees. It needs to be repeated three times before proceeding to the next step.

3. An area of responsibility should not be difficult to define. As the project manager, you need to develop a concise definition of which team members or subgroups will be responsible for a range of tasks. Arrive at this definition through three methods:

   a. *Type of Work.* A specific activity requires exposure to the sources of specific types of information. Certain team members

Figure A-1. Loops between two team members.

Team Member 1

a. Prepare an outline of task and give it to team member 2.

b. Team member 2 asks for clarification. Review the outline and clarify.

Team Member 2

a. Check the outline submitted by team member 1.

b. Is the outline clear? If not, ask team member 1 for help.

c. When team member 1 has answered your question, return to previous step (check outline).

d. The outline is clear. Proceed to the next step.

e. Prepare a flowchart summarizing the steps in this procedure.

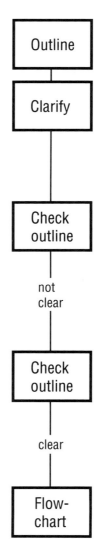

will have experience or expertise. For example, accounting employees are capable of working with numerical analysis and research, whereas marketing employees are more suited to market-related activities.

b. *Individuals.* Certain team members are selected because of their experience and knowledge, especially if demonstrated on past projects or within your department. For example, you know that one person has the ability to organize a large body of information; that person would be a valuable team member if your project required that talent.

c. *Phases.* Some phases of your project dictate the types of employees needed to execute them. For example, an employee with systems analysis training would be a valuable team member for a project involving the design and implementation of new software.

Chapter 11

1. Review involves the same elements in projects and departments. However, because the project is short term, it demands more concise definition and follow-through. The three issues involved are:

a. *Defining a Standard for Performance.* Team members are expected to play a precise role in your project, so you need to provide them with guidelines for achieving the outcome you expect. This extends beyond schedule and budget requirements. Standards should include guidelines for quality of results, cooperation between team members, and the final result.

b. *Finding Appropriate Applications of the Standard.* You need to develop a testing method for review and then determine what each test reveals. You measure and judge performance consistently only if you have a clear standard against which to make determinations.

c. *Deciding What Actions (if Any) You Must Take.* Upon completing your periodic review, do you need to correct problems, either existing or anticipated? You may need to identify problems underlying scheduling delays related to teamwork, morale, or ability.

2. The project, unlike your department, involves a group of people who do not work together regularly. Their roles may not be well defined. Review is a constant requirement because problems can arise unexpectedly. The exceptional nature of projects places an added demand on you and your team that is not commonplace in the department.

3. When reporting to management on the status of your project, include these sections in your report:

a. A brief description of the project

b. The current status of the schedule and budget

c. Explanations where needed (i.e., reserve this section for explanations of unsolved problems; don't take up space unnecessarily)

d. Your expectations for the future (e.g., Will the project be completed on time and within budget? If not, what are the causes, and what can be done to overcome this problem? What delays, if any, do you anticipate to face between now and completion?)

Chapter 12

1. Establishing and maintaining communication with your core team members is difficult in and of itself. In addition, you must keep open the lines of communication with others, including:

a. *The Assignment.* The executive who gave you the assignment may have a far different idea about what your project is meant to achieve. Only by ensuring that you are both on the same track will you be able to complete your assignment as expected. A second problem arises when the project's scope or definition are changed after you have started, which might occur without your being told. You are more likely to be told of any such changes if you keep in touch with your superiors.

American Management Association
www.amanet.org

b. ***Other Departments.*** You cannot expect managers of other departments to adopt your project priorities at the expense of continuing work in their department. The department manager lives with a set of priorities, too, so your project takes second place. You can resolve many difficulties throughout the project by keeping this important point in mind.

c. ***Outside Resources.*** When you need the participation of other divisions, subsidiaries, vendors, or consultants, you need to remember this important reality: Your priorities aren't shared by others. They will not always appreciate the urgency of your requests or the importance of your deadlines.

2. Approach the communication challenge in dealing with other departments with a checklist of steps, which includes:

a. ***Visiting the Other Manager Before You Finalize the Schedule.*** Make sure your proposed schedule will not cause conflicts for the other manager. Be willing to make adjustments when problems arise. Include the manager in your decision to improve communication and cooperation.

b. ***Keeping in Touch While the Project Is Under Way.*** The communication task is not limited to the early phases only. Communicate regularly with all department managers whose employees are part of your team.

c. ***Working with the Manager to Anticipate Problems.*** Think of the other department as a team member, never as an adversary. Just as individuals split their time between their department and your project, the department is being asked to split its resources between its priorities and yours.

d. ***Remaining as Flexible as Possible.*** Other departments face unexpected demands and scheduling problems for their work. This could affect your ability to stay on schedule, especially if employees are prevented from working on your project as a result. Maintain flexibility and understand that department managers cannot anticipate the unexpected; your schedule and use of resources is subject to constant revision.

e. *Confronting the Problem, Not the People.* When dealing with outside departments, you can expect conflicts to arise in some form. Try to speak directly with managers to resolve these problems. Avoid confronting people, which is counterproductive. Instead, emphasize the problem and how you can work together to resolve it.

3. Set goals and express them as part of your agenda. Encourage action-oriented discussions and resolutions, and don't allow your meetings to end without resolving the problems. Your objectives should be to:

a. *Express the goals of your project.* These define and add context to every discussion. They keep everyone on the subject at hand so your agenda isn't sidetracked.

b. *Explain the level of team commitment you need.* Even when conflicts between project and department arise, it is possible to arrive at a compromise that solves the problem.

c. *Specify deadlines for phases and final completion.* If deadlines are not taken seriously in your company, it's probably because they are missed most of the time. In a project, though, each phase deadline is critical. Phase deadlines and your final project deadline should be considered important.

d. *Identify "critical" phases that must be completed before the next step can begin*. Prepare a network diagram and identify these pivotal periods during the project. Remember, delays in critical phases have the greatest impact, because they prevent the project from proceeding.

e. *Point out the likely problem areas.* Remember to be proactive in anticipating and preventing problems.

f. *Agree on priorities for your project*. Make sure that every team member knows what is expected and what the project is supposed to accomplish.

Chapter 13

1. Leadership action in a project environment is not the same as that in a department. Projects are exceptions, have finite lives, and may involve people who do not normally report to you. Organize your project with these actions:

    a. ***Define the goals and purpose of the project.*** It could take considerable effort to pin down management to the point of definition, yet this step is essential if the project is to succeed.

    b. ***Organize a schedule.*** A complex project with many phases and a large team has to be organized carefully. Use your initial schedule to locate potential trouble spots, and devise solutions before your schedule is finalized.

    c. ***Develop a team approach.*** When you bring your team together, encourage each member to take an active role in developing the schedule, meeting deadlines, and observing the budget.

    d. ***Resolve conflicts.*** Problems arise, either due to scheduling delays or personality clashes. You need to anticipate these problems and resolve them diplomatically.

    e. ***Keep the lines of communication open.*** Be continually aware of the overall network affecting your project. Team members, outside resources, other departments, and top management are all involved, and you need to remain in touch with everyone.

    f. ***Meet budgets and deadlines.*** The project is judged by standards of performance—namely, the budget and the schedule. Making a sincere effort to meet these standards defines your capabilities as a project manager.

    g. ***Train and supervise team members.*** You function not only in the role of controller and organizer, but also as the project supervisor. Ensure that all team members know their assignments and how to proceed. Provide all of the supervision and training each person requires.

2. As a successful project manager, you need to master these skills:

    a. Understanding and practicing the team approach

    b. Applying a standard that isn't necessarily the same as you'd apply in your department

    c. Organizing a multiple-level effort

d. Remaining flexible when it comes to scheduling, priorities, and assignments

e. Communicating with all affected people and departments

3. No single series of rules or standards applies to every project. Among the variables that will affect your style are:

a. *The Makeup of the Team.* If your team comes exclusively from your department, it is not difficult to operate the project. The real test comes when you need to work with team members from outside your department.

b. *Scope of the Project.* As you might expect, longer-term projects with larger, more diverse teams are more difficult to coordinate. Thus, the ideas you employ to define, organize, and monitor your project should be altered based on the project's scope and composition.

c. *Cooperation From Other Departments.* If you establish and maintain clear lines of communication and keep other managers informed, you minimize possible problem areas. However, no matter how much effort you give, you have no guarantee that other managers will cooperate. Conflict may still occur, and they'll vary based on your management style and on the motives and interests of other managers.

d. *Time Demands.* Deadlines are the norm, and coordinating them with the desire for quality is the difficult part. Style has to take a lower priority in crunch situations.

Glossary

area of responsibility The specific person, department, or other resource responsible for the execution of a task or process as part of
the project; a team member or stakeholder involved in the project
and its execution or in a process that is the subject of the project.

assumptions The underlying set of beliefs supporting a budget, schedule, or other effort involving calculation of future requirements;
referred to in order to identify the causes of variances in budgets
or time.

bar chart A chart based on a series of bars representing value or time,
and prepared vertically or horizontally; the Gantt chart is a type of
bar chart used to track the planned and actual schedules of project
phases.

budget An estimate of the costs and expenses involved in the project;
the financial road map used to monitor and control expenses of
the project; the means of the financial monitoring of a project and
a measurement of success based on planned and actual costs and
expenses.

budget variance The outcome when the actual expenses of a project
are higher (unfavorable) or lower (favorable) than the budgeted
amount for the same time period.

Business Process Management (BPM) A process used to describe
how work flows through the organization in a series of steps; the
basis for preparation of a flowchart and for assigning tasks and
processes among the project team.

control (a) The action of monitoring a process to reduce errors or to
improve productivity; (b) a system designed to improve processing
in terms of time and quality.

Critical Path Method (CPM) Method for tracking processes through a
series of network paths and involving multiple participants, includ-

ing start and end dates for each segment of the overall process; a visualization of the project schedule.

decision loop A pattern within a process in which a decision may result in the process's continuing or being sent back to be fixed, repeated, or checked.

decision tree A visual tool in either outline or flowchart format used to analyze various outcomes of a proposed course of action; analyzes probable outcomes and the cost or benefit of each alternative.

diagram/narrative combination A technique for describing a process or task, in which a series of steps are shown via flowchart boxes and accompanied with written explanations.

DMAIC The action plan in a Six Sigma project, whose initials represent five specific steps: define, measure, analyze, improve, control.

Failure Mode and Effects Analysis (FMEA) The process of determining precisely what can go wrong and deciding how to reduce it, a concept used in Six Sigma–based project analysis; a risk management and prevention aspect of the Six Sigma approach to project management.

favorable variance The condition when actual expenses are lower than budgeted for a specified period of time or activity (project phase, for example).

flowchart A visual representation of a schedule prepared with great detail and in vertical or horizontal form; identifies the process, the responsible department or person (area of responsibility), and time requirements, and highlights potential weak links.

Gantt chart A type of scheduling chart named for its originator Henry Gantt; each phase is shown on a vertical plane from start to finish; also visually demonstrates phases that overlap. Additionally, planned and actual phase outcomes can be distinguished with the use of color variation (for example, white boxes representing the plan and black boxes the actual).

horizontal flowchart A type of flowchart representing the processing of information from left to right, including different rows for each area of responsibility and time requirements for each task or phase; the network diagram of a project.

loop A point within a process in which the path may need to be re-

peated based on one of three criteria: verification, decision, or repetition.

network diagram A left-to-right flowchart showing tasks, area of responsibility, and time requirements for a project.

process owner In Six Sigma projects, the individual or department
that benefits from an improved process or system or that is involved directly with the input, processing, or output.

Program Evaluation and Review Technique (PERT) A diagramming
system employed for project scheduling, in which time requirements are weighted to graphically demonstrate the overall time demands for the project and its phases.

quality control Any procedure designed to improve and maintain the
highest possible level of quality and reduction of defects in a process. Systems such as Six Sigma are formalized varieties of quality
control efforts.

repetition loop A pattern within a process in which completed tasks
are moved forward to the next step and incomplete tasks are returned for further processing.

risk management The controls, planning, and preventive measures
required to address and prevent threats, known or unknown,
through specific measures: insurance, transfer, mitigation, and
transfer.

schedule The document prepared by the project team to map out the
steps in the project and to track progress toward a specified completion date; the means for controlling the overall time and deadline issues of a project, used to anticipate time delays and to take
steps to avoid them.

SIPOC A process map used in Six Sigma projects to describe the chain
of events that include five key elements: suppliers, input, process,
output, and customers.

Six Sigma A quality control and project management system designed
to quantify processes in terms of the rate of defects and, in addition, to train personnel within an organization in broad-based team
attitudes. Defects are quantified by the study of the statistical value
of sigma (σ) in order to track improvements in processes through
the reduction of defects and variances. A six sigma is as close as

possible to a defect-free process, with fewer than four defects per million operations.

stakeholder Any department, company, or individual with a direct interest in the project and its outcome.

standard deviation A statistical calculation used to estimate the rate of defects in an operation; the standard used to identify the change in defects used in Six Sigma projects.

tabular format A WBS-based method for outlining a project by phase and task, in which vertical breakdown is developed, often as a preliminary step in developing more detailed flowcharts.

unfavorable variance The condition when actual expenses are higher than the budget for a specified period of time or activity (project phase, for example).

value chain A concept defining levels of both quality control and process management, used to ensure both quality and value as part of the improved final result.

verification loop A pattern within a process in which an outcome is checked; if the result is correct, the process continues and if it is not, the outcome is returned to be revised.

Voice of the Customer (VOC) In Six Sigma projects, an overlay of customer requirements as part of defining the project and its goals.

weak links Locations within a process where errors or defects are most likely to occur, usually found when processes are passed from one area of responsibility to another; identifying weak links is the key to deciding where control emphasis should be focused to make projects more effective.

Work Breakdown Structure (WBS) A system used to list and identify the specific task involved in the project, by way of flowcharts or outlines; the WBS is designed to ensure that all tasks and phases are included in the schedule and that these are planned out in a rational sequence for execution.

Index